By WILLIAM H. DANFORTH
Chairman of the Board,
Ralston Purina Company,
Checkerboard Square,
St. Louis, Mo.

FOUR-FOLD DEVELOPMENT

Think Tall

Stand Tall Smile Tall

Live Tall

FIFTEENTH EDITION
PRIVATELY PRINTED FOR MY PERSONAL FRIENDS
AND DARING YOUTH WHO MAY CROSS MY PATH.
MAY, 1953

By William H. Danforth

■ ■ ■

As a Man Thinketh

As a Man Doeth

Adventures in Achievement

Fight

Action

Growth

Power

Sidelights From France, Spain, Africa

Highlights From Europe

Russia Under the Hammer and Sickle

Random Ramblings in India

I Dare You

Four Golden Keys

Around the World

Fifteenth Edition
Copyright, 1953, by William H. Danforth
St. Louis, Missouri
Printed in U. S. A.

By WILLIAM H. DANFORTH

Chairman of the Board,
Ralston Purina Company,
Checkerboard Square,
St. Louis, Mo.

FOUR-FOLD DEVELOPMENT

Think Tall

Stand Tall Smile Tall

Live Tall

Martino Fine Books
Eastford, CT
2017

Martino Fine Books
P.O. Box 913,
Eastford, CT 06242 USA

ISBN 978-1-68422-079-3

Copyright 2017
Martino Fine Books

Cover Design Tiziana Matarazzo

Printed in the United States of America On 100% Acid-Free Paper

FOREWORD

THOSE OF US who have been associated with Mr. Danforth in business know this Dare idea works. Practically all the leaders in his great organization were boys who came from humble surroundings and were dared by him to high accomplishments. He has dared most by his own daring example. Mr. Danforth gives the best that is in him, whether he is guiding a great industry, traveling in a remote corner of the world, shooting ducks or playing with his grandchildren. The day ahead is always the most thrilling day in his life. The job at hand is always the most important one he has ever undertaken. He never gives less than his best.

Several years ago Mr. Danforth published "I Dare You" in a limited first edition for the benefit of his business, family and personal friends. Each book passed many times from one person to another. The idea spread and affected people of all ages and in all walks of life. In one case, "I Dare You" inspired the sale of over $5,000,000 worth of insurance in a special day of the Life Underwriters' Association. The demand from salesmanagers, Y. M. C. A. secretaries, business executives, college organizations, vocational teachers, personnel workers, preachers—everyone whose aim it is to challenge men and women to superior accomplishment—soon exhausted the early editions. Now comes the fifteenth edition revised and improved. "I Dare You" is in its second printing in Canada. Here is more than a book. It is a working pattern of life written out of a pioneer business man's own rich experience. It is the challenge for which Today's Youth is waiting. It is a practical plan of action for everybody who wants to go somewhere and be somebody.

G. M. PHILPOTT

iii

AUTHOR'S PREFACE

I agree that a business man should stick to business. But a proven four-fold program, plus a love for Youth, plus an inner urge—all *dare* me to write this book.

"I Dare You" is for the daring few who are headed somewhere. Those afraid to Dare might as well pass it up. It will weary the lazy because it calls for immediate action. It will bore the sophisticated, and amuse the skeptics. It will antagonize others. Some will not even know what it is all about. It will not be over popular because it calls for courage, swift and daring. But in the eyes of you, one of *the priceless few*, I trust will come a gleam of battle as you read on. You can be a bigger person than you are and I am going to prove it to you.

I am indebted beyond measure to Gordon M. Philpott who has been of inestimable help in the writing and editing of "I Dare You." His keen insight, his rare judgment and his frank criticisms have helped make this book a labor of love instead of a drab task. I honor him as a close associate in business, but most of all I cherish him as an understanding friend.

W. H. D.

TABLE OF CONTENTS

I DARE YOU!

"What I've dared I've willed;
And what I've willed, I'll do!"
—*Melville*

I DARE YOU!

It is difficult to put a challenge on paper. I would rather look you straight in the eye and say, "I dare you!" In my mind that's exactly what I am doing. I am on one side of a table. You are on the other. I am looking across and saying "I dare you!"

I Dare You, young man, you who come from a home poverty—I dare you to have the qualities of a Lincoln.

I Dare You, heir of wealth and proud ancestry, with your generations of worthy stock, your traditions of leadership—I dare you to achieve something that will make the future point to you with even more pride than the present is pointing to those who have gone before you.

I Dare You, young mother, to make your life a masterpiece upon which that little family of yours can build. Strong women bring forth strong men.

I Dare You, debutante, to be a queen. Make life obey you, not you it. It is only a shallow dare to do the foolish things. I dare you to do the uplifting, courageous things.

I Dare You, young executive, to shoulder more responsibility joyously, to launch out into the deep, to build magnificently.

I Dare You, young author, to win the Nobel prize.

I Dare You, young researcher, to become a Microbe Hunter.

I Dare You, barefoot boy on the farm, to become a Master Farmer—A Hunger Fighter.

I Dare You, man of affairs, to have a "Magnificent Obsession."

I Dare You, Grandfather, with your roots deep in the soil and your head above the crowd, catching the rays of the sun, to plan a daring program to crown the years of your life.

I Dare You, who think life is humdrum, to start a fight. I dare you who are weak to be strong; you who are dull to be sparkling; you who are slaves to be kings.

I Dare You, whoever you are, to share with others the fruits of your daring. Catch a passion for helping others and a richer life will come back to you!

"Ye are the salt of the earth;
Ye are the light of the world."
—*From the Sermon on the Mount*

YOU CAN BE BIGGER
THAN YOU ARE

As a small boy, before the time of drainage ditches, I lived in the country surrounded by swamp lands. Those were days of chills and fever and malaria. When I came to the city to school, I was sallow-cheeked and hollow-chested. One of my teachers, George Warren Krall, was what we then called a health crank. We laughed at his ideas. They went in one ear and came out the other. But George Warren Krall never let up. One day he seemed to single me out personally. With flashing eye and in tones that I will never forget, he looked straight at me and said, "I dare you to be the healthiest boy in the class."

That brought me up with a jar. Around me were boys all stronger and more robust than I. To be the healthiest boy in the class when I was thin and sallow and imagined at least that I was full of swamp poisons!—the man was crazy. But I was brought up to take dares. His voice went on. He pointed directly at me. "I dare you to chase those chills and fevers out of your system. I dare you to fill your body with fresh air, pure water, wholesome food, and daily exercise until your cheeks are rosy, your chest full, and your limbs sturdy."

As he talked something seemed to happen inside me. My blood was up. It answered the dare and surged all through my body into tingling finger tips as though itching for battle.

I chased the poisons out of my system. I built a body that has equalled the strongest boys in that class, and has outlived and outlasted most of them. Since that day I haven't lost any time on account of sickness. You can imagine how often I have blessed that teacher who dared a sallow-cheeked boy to be the healthiest in the class.

Several years later, Henry Woods, one of our promising boys, pushed through the door of my office early one morning and stood facing me defiantly.

"I'm quitting," he said.

"What's the trouble, Henry?"

"Just this, I'm no salesman. I haven't got the nerve. I haven't got the ability, and I'm not worth the money you are paying me."

There was something splendid about the courage of a man who would so frankly admit failure to his boss. He couldn't do that without nerve. Suddenly my mind recalled that boyhood scene when a teacher dared a hollow-chested youngster to be strong. To Henry's surprise, instead of accepting his resignation, I looked him squarely in the eye and said:

"If I know how to pick men, you have sales stuff in you. *I dare you, Henry Woods, to get out of this office, right now, and come back tonight with more orders than you have ever sold in any one day in your whole life.*"

He looked at me dumbfounded. Then a flash came into his eyes. It must have been the light of battle—the same something that had surged through me years before in answer to the teacher's dare. He turned and walked out of my office.

That night he came back. The defiant look of the early morning was replaced by the glow of victory. He had made the best record of his life. He had beaten his best—and he has been beating his best ever since. Incidentally, I'll give you a secret of his life. In his quiet way he is one of the best helpers of young salesmen I ever knew. He thrives by giving his experience to others. The world is full of men like Henry Woods just waiting for a Dare.

Up in the American Youth Foundation Camps each summer I come into contact with hundreds of young people who possess qualities of leadership. A few years ago a young fellow, who was working as a mechanic in a large electrical firm, came to me much perplexed. He had been forced to go to work when he had finished high school. Later he saw boys with technical college training outstrip him. Sensing he had ability to be much more than a mechanic, I dared him to leave his job and go back to school. Again I saw that priceless light of battle leap into the eyes of a fighter. He had no money, but, somehow, he got to college, was graduated with honors, and today the might-have-been mechanic is a prominent electrical engineer. I can tell you one of the secrets of his life, too . . . he keeps on growing by sharing, because now he has a mania for helping others get an education.

These are brief pages taken from the book of my practical experiences. There are scores of other pages like them. Unfortunately, however, there are many pages that would tell that other story of those who have been dared to do the super thing, but in whose eyes the light of battle failed to gleam. But the "I Dare You" plan *has* worked with thousands. It will work with you. As your first step, I Dare You to read this book through tonight before you go to bed. Don't stop. Hurry through just to get its *feel*. Then if you are determined to be one of those priceless few leaders who are destined to reach the top, take this book as a program for adventuring toward your highest possibilities.

ARE YOU ONE OF THE PRICELESS FEW?

I am on a voyage of discovery. I search for those of you who will go on a great adventure. I am looking for you, one of the audacious few, who will face life courageously, ready to strike straight at the heart of anything that is keeping you from your best; you intrepid ones behind whom the world moves forward. To you, I am going to unfold a secret power that but few know how to use—the secret power of daring and sharing which carries with it tremendous responsibilities. Once you have it, you can never be the same again. Once it is yours, you can never rest until you have given it to others. And the more you give away the greater becomes your capacity to give. Deep down in the very fibre of your being you must light an urge that can never be put out. It will catch this side of your life, then that side. It will widen your horizon. It will light up unknown reserves and discover new capacities for living and growing. It will become, if you don't look out, a mighty conflagration that will consume your every waking hour. And to its blazing glory a thousand other lives will come for light and warmth and power.

It is going to take courage to let this urge possess you. My life in business and my contacts with young people have convinced me that the world is full of unused talents and latent ability. The reason these talents lie buried is that the individual hasn't the courage to dig them up and use them. Everybody should be doing better than he is, but only a few dare. Prospectors for gold tell us that gold is where they find it. It may be in the bed of a river or on the mountain top. And prospectors for courage tell us the same thing. The one who dares may be found in a cottage or in a castle. But wherever you live, whoever you are, whatever you have or have not—if you dare, you are challenged to enlist in a great cause.

H. G. Wells tells how every human being can determine whether he has really succeeded in life. He says: "Wealth, notoriety, place, and power are no measure of success whatever. The only true measure of success is the ratio between what we might have done and what we might have been on the one hand, and the thing we have made and the thing we have made of ourselves on the other."

I want you to start a crusade in your life—to dare to be your best. I maintain that you are a better, more capable person than you have demonstrated so far. The only reason you are not the person you should be is you don't dare to be. Once you dare, once you stop drifting with the crowd and face life courageously, life takes on a new significance. New forces take shape within you. New powers harness themselves for your service.

Who wants to do unimportant and uninteresting things? Who even wants to gratify an ambition that has grown into a passion for fame and fortune? To desire something permanent in life, to develop your gifts to the largest possible use—that's your dare. You have a wealth of possibilities, but maybe up to this time you have lacked a definite aim. You have a gun and plenty of ammunition. Now I dare you to aim at something worthy of the best that is in you.

My practical experience has convinced me that inner growth and broadening personality come from daring and sharing. You dare to use the talents you have. You find yourself growing stronger— physically, mentally, socially, and spiritually. You multiply your daring a hundred-fold by sharing its fruits. You give your life away and, behold! a richer life comes back to you. This principle works through all of life:

Our most valuable possessions are those which can be shared without lessening: those which, when shared, multiply. Our least valuable possessions are those which when divided are diminished.

Old or young, rich or poor, man or woman, if you are one of those audacious few willing to dare and then to share—then come with me. This book is written for you. I promise you adventure. I promise you a more abundant life.

> "All who joy would win
> Must share it. Happiness was born a twin."

I DARE YOU TO ADVENTURE

Before we start on the great adventure, let's be dead sure we want to take it. Unless one is interested and enthusiastic he would not even want to go on a picnic, let alone start on a journey destined to bulk large in life's affairs. When our appetites have a sharp edge, we enjoy our meals.

Adventure means living to the full.

You will want to start when you know how much happiness it will bring you. Some of my young friends, who are freedom-loving pleasure seekers, maintain that drifting along with life is happiness, that resistance is vulgar, that self-indulgence is self-expression. Rot! I take issue with them. The line of least resistance makes crooked rivers and crooked men. Each fish that battles upstream is worth ten that loaf in lazy bays.

True, the mass of people prefer the easy way. Old ways require no effort. Physically or mentally lazy people do not want to adjust themselves. But they have never tasted the thrill of victory. I remember once during the first World War a captain was wounded in No Man's Land when returning from a raid. Snipers and machine gunners shot across a defiant barrage as though daring anyone to come and get his prostrate body. The company commander called for two volunteers to undertake the dangerous mission of rescuing the wounded man. The whole company stepped forward. The major chose the two men with the most deserving record and longest service. Out on their bellies they crawled and brought in their captain. In crack regiments it is a privilege to dare and to give. There are no big thrills in the trenches. But just poke your head over the parapet and you'll find excitement enough. Your days won't be humdrum when you lift your head above the crowd.

"I *Dare* You to Adventure" is my message to those red-blooded young leaders I meet e v e r y summer at the A m e r i c a n Youth Foundation Camp up in Michigan. Every year there come to this camp hundreds and hundreds of boys and girls, young men and young women, who aspire to be leaders. During certain hours, the whole Camp resounds with the keen competition these young people have in striving to best one another in a game of baseball, in a diving contest, or in climbing to some lofty height. Or at another time of the day they are just as intense, just as interested in a mental training program—because these young people are to be future leaders and their trained directors have learned the art of making their mental program just as interesting and absorbing as their physical program. At night in the council circle each tribe competes against each other in entertainment features. Each future leader learns the art of expressing himself, entertaining his fellow

campers; he handles his personality in such a way
it attracts, leads and influences others. During a
devotional program these hundreds of young people
are just as absorbed in expressing and developing
their spiritual selves as they are on the athletic
field or in the study room or in the council circle.
These young campers have realized that all sides of
life can be equally interesting. Show me boys and
girls anywhere who enjoy life more than do these.
"My own self, at my very best, all the time," is the
Camp Motto. They are daring to live at their best,
following a Four-square program, and they are
having a glorious time doing it. Living right has a
lasting kick in it. Living wrong is a bit of foam on
top, that's all.*

In the spirit of a crusader, life is a glorious adventure. If you jump out of bed in the morning full of
fight, daring people or circumstances to depress you,
you are on the road to victory. If you face problems
aggressively, they are half solved already. If you
aspire to larger responsibilities, they will meet you
half way.

But how to dare, you ask. That is coming. First,
it is necessary to agree that living aggressively
changes the whole complexion of life. So many are
preys to fear. You fear losing your job. You fear
sickness or hard times or failure. But remember,
courage is not the absence of fear, it is the conquest
of it. Not until you dare to attack will you master
your fears.

And why dare? Because unless you dare you cannot win. Deep down in every heart is the desire to be somebody, to get somewhere. But so often we sit waiting for the opportunity. I have found opportunities do not come to those who wait. They are captured by those who attack.

Perhaps you are sitting back in your chair reading this and saying, "It is all very well for him to say that. But my circumstances are different. It is impossible for me to dare." I challenge that thought in your mind. I know it is your deadly enemy. Because of it, you, more than others, must dare. The humdrum life is the one most in need of adventure. You can cure your weakness by vigorous action. Start something! Break a window, if necessary.

I am daring you to think bigger, to act bigger, and to be bigger. And I am promising you a richer life and a more exciting life if you do. I am showing you a world teeming with opportunity. The rewards for daring were never so rich or so plentiful. Science, religion, business, education—all are looking for the man who dares face life, to attack rather than defend.

Before you read further, be honest with yourself. What do you think of life, anyway? What do you think of yourself? Are you satisfied that you are carrying responsibility equal to your capacity? Are you contented to have posterity look at your life so far and say, "That is all he was capable of?" Or, are you one of the priceless few, one of those with a restless feeling that some day you are going to climb to your rightful place of leadership? That some day you are going to create something worthy of your best? If this is your attitude then my voyage of discovery is not in vain. You are the volunteer for whom I am looking. Then make that "some day" you have been waiting for, today.

*The American Youth Foundation Christian Leadership Camps include a five week period—ages 12 to 15 for younger boys and a similar period for younger girls; also a two weeks training period, ages 16 to 21 for older boys and a similar period for older girls. For particulars, address American Youth Foundation, 3930 Lindell Boulevard, St. Louis, Missouri.

I DARE YOU TO DO THINGS

In France, during those dark days of 1918, I marveled at the way my old army comrade, Colonel E. L. Daley of the Sixth Engineers, got things done. I began to understand better when I heard what he had said to his own boys in America when he was bidding them goodbye. "Boys," said he, "your name is Daley, and Daley stands for *the ability to do things!*" No longer will you step aside to let crusaders go by. Others shall step aside for you because *you* are now a crusader. You have the ability to do things. You know where you are going. The world makes way for the man who knows where he is going. Streets are crowded, traffic is jammed—a fire engine is coming—everything makes way for it. True, moments of weakness and depression and laziness are going to assail you. But that is the time for battle. One forward step—one swift constructive action—will send these enemies scurrying to cover.

I remembered reading a newspaper account of a mother killing a bear with an axe when it threatened her baby. A woman cannot kill a bear—but she did.

Gordon Philpott tells me of a Canadian street car conductor, who rose to be a General in the first

World War. The conductor did not know he could command men—but he could.

Not many years ago a young man was working as a section hand on a railroad. His thoroughness won him an opportunity to work for a few days in the shipping office. During those few days the superintendent asked the young substitute clerk for some vital facts and figures. The young man did not know anything about bookkeeping, but he worked three days and three nights without sleep and had the facts ready when the superintendent returned. The same daring which made him always willing to tackle the bigger job even though he knew nothing about it—the same thoroughness which has characterized everything he has done, have been stepping stones to higher and higher responsibilities. Today he is vice-president of our own company.

Until he was nineteen, a young Kentucky mountain boy had never been out of his own county and had never seen a railroad. He rose to become Chairman of the Board of one of our largest Western banks and a Past-President of the American Bankers' Association. In time he was elected a Trustee of Berea College, that marvelous Kentucky school of three thousand mountain boys and girls. "This is the greatest honor of my life," said this now grown-up country boy, in humbly accepting this place of service and responsibility. Experience had taught him that real satisfaction is not riches or fame but in giving one's self for others.

An Alabama miner, working with his hands, realized the lack of an education. He studied by candle light. He "read" law a bit. When gold was struck in the Yukon, he was swept off his feet. He dared to go. In the Yukon he found his fortune in the bowels of the earth. He also found something far greater. Lost in a driving snow storm, in this cold, bleak Northland, he saw in the distance a shining cross set up by the missionaries and that vision dared him to follow a new Master. He found a new Life. Today he is one of our most magnetic speakers and is investing his fortune and himself in Christian work.

The other day I saw a creative country boy, supposedly lacking in culture, poise, and social graces, hold his own in a brilliant gathering—to his own amazement, as well as mine.

I know a successful but modest business man, who, when called on in an emergency, discovered in himself a rich capacity for spiritual uplift to those around him.

I can give you all these men's names. I know them well. They found they had capacity and used it.

Wars and emergencies discover many unopened doors in people's lives. Why not declare War? Why not put a bomb under your capacities? Why not force a crisis? Without some such incentives to stir souls to action, the mother never knows her strength, the street car conductor never discovers the General, the section hand, the miner, the country boys, the business man, live and die without realizing the sleeping giants within them. The purpose of this book is, first, to help you discover what

living tools you have to work with, and, secondly, to
dare you to use all of them. Launch out into the
deep. Walter B. Pitkin, author of "The Psychology
of Achievement," says that thousands of young
people can double, treble, and quadruple their
effectiveness simply by being aroused to Creative
Audacity. But, alas, many lack courage because at a
still deeper level, they lack the immense energies
which a daring program demands. He tells me that
he used to train boxers and often he would find a
brilliantly clever boxer fail to rise in the sport—"he
lacked the punch" because he showed physical
fatigue long before less skilled rivals did—and in
the long gruelling run lost.

It is a tragedy indeed to see an ambitious person
striving after some goal he has neither the energy
nor ability to reach. But it is a thousand times
greater tragedy and, alas, a more common one, to
see Generals and Vice-Presidents, spiritual and
mental leaders, passing by unnoticed as street car
conductors, section hands, and bell hops.

But what is it, you ask, that turns a street car
conductor into a General? What is the method? Did
he just go to the War, dare to become a General,
then stick out his chest and wait for the medals to
be pinned on? No, sir! Generals aren't made that
way. The fact is, several things took place inside
that street car conductor before he became a General. Before the War, he had been living in a narrow
conductor world—eating, sleeping, mingling with
a few friends and collecting fares. Suddenly he
stepped into a new world. Horizons were pushed

back on all sides. The sleeping giants within him
stirred and awakened.

What were these sleeping giants? The first was a
physical one. Where he had spent most of his waking
hours in the stuffy, stodgy atmosphere of a street
car, he now galloped about on a horse, had physical
instructors punch in his stomach and push up his
chest, got plenty of exercise, lived out of doors, ate
simple food. He found vibrant health and abundant
strength at his disposal. Then his mental life broad-
ened. He bunked in a tent next to a college professor. He worked on a gun crew beside a civil
engineer. Their minds quickened his. He saw the
great cities of London and Paris. He went to an
artillery school and found he could learn to do
higher mathematics as well as add up fares. He had
only needed to use one corner of his brain to be a
conductor. Now almost every new experience
demanded that another compartment be opened
and aired. In the third place, he had the gift of
making all kinds of people like him—men and boys
in the army from every walk of life, fighting with a
great purpose in their hearts. Back at home his
street car contacts were only of the meagerest sort.
One priceless day he discovered that he had a new
power—the ability to lead people. Laborers, college
men, business men recognized him as the one to
march in front. A street car conductor never had
that opportunity. He was always in the rear. And,
finally, although he never made any religious pro-
fession, for the first time in his life he was filled
with a passion for a great moral cause.

But why, you ask, didn't all the other street car conductors become Generals? They were thrown into the same environment. The answer is obvious. Either they didn't have the capacity to be a General, or they didn't *dare* to use the capacity they had. This one found within himself undreamed of physical powers, unused mental gifts, decided ability to influence people, and a depth of character which was the rock on which his success was built. And, having discovered this four-sided life, he had the courage and daring to make it broaden, deepen, and rise above the lives of those around him.

The same is true of the country boy who was nineteen before he saw a railroad. But he made up his mind that some day he would ride in the cars and see the world. Only a country boy? Yes, but with the capacity of a man able to carry world problems on his shoulders. For nineteen years on the farm he had been building a strong physical foundation. Then, when opportunity came, he found each successive year developing mental, social, and spiritual resources, until he received the highest honor in the banking world.

What are the hidden resources to look for? What are these sleeping giants within us? There are four of them—the physical, the mental, the social, and the spiritual. Life cannot be complete unless we develop all four sides. Each side that is developed in turn stimulates the other three sides. "All for one and one for all." Life's Musketeers work together for one common end. All down the pages of history great lives have been telling us this secret of the four-fold life. Pick them out of any age, from any line of endeavor. They all tell the same story—that progress is a complete program coming out of all four sides of life. St. Luke gives us eloquent evidence by just one little peep into the four-fold development of the greatest success of all time: "And Jesus increased in wisdom and stature and in favor with God and man."

Now listen to Sir Wilfred Grenfell's message: "Man must play, work, love and worship to get the most out of life." Read his words again.

How dare you have within yourself these four-fold capacities and not use them?

That is the first principle that I want thoroughly to fix in your mind—that life is a four-sided affair—that your daring program is going to lead you into physical adventures, mental adventures, social adventures, spiritual adventures. You have not one, but four lives to live—a four-fold opportunity to grow. A body, a brain, a heart, and a soul—these are our living tools. To use them is not a task. It is a golden opportunity. To find new capacities within you is not robbing you of any pleasure. It is bringing new treasures into every waking hour. It is helping you touch life at all angles, absorb strength from all contacts, pour out power on all fronts.

And here is another interesting thing. The more you pour out, the more you find to pour. The more of Life's treasures you keep to yourself, the less you have. The more you share with others, the more you have yourself. One of Life's great rules is this: The more you give, the more you get. I am not trying to soar in the clouds. This principle is the result of my own practical experience. I know that if you dare to use the talents you have you find yourself growing stronger physically, mentally, socially, spiritually, and that you multiply them a hundred-fold by sharing their fruits. You give your life away and behold! a richer life comes back to you.

I repeat Life's great principle. *Our most valuable possessions are those which can be shared without lessening; those which when shared multiply. Our least valuable possessions are those which when divided are diminished.*

NOW FOR THE START

Suppose you were to draw a picture of your life as you are living it today. How near four-square would it be?

Would it look like this?

or this?

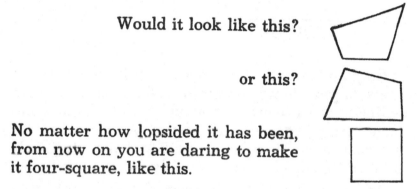

No matter how lopsided it has been, from now on you are daring to make it four-square, like this.

I have been taught that a pencil and a piece of paper help clarify the mind. I want so to burn this four-square idea into your brain that it will be a part of you. I won't be able to put across the completeness of the four-square life unless I get you to make definite moves for yourself.

On the left, at the top of the next page, I have drawn my four square checker. Now won't you take a sheet of paper and draw yours? Make all sides equal. Write "Physical" on the left-hand side, "Mental" at the top and "Social" on the right-hand side, "Religious" under the base. Then in the middle write "My Checker" and sign your initials.

MENTAL

PHYSICAL

SOCIAL

RELIGIOUS

No plan is worth the paper it is printed on unless it starts you doing something. There is too much telling in this life and not enough doing. Unless you have actually drawn and labeled your checker for yourself, even though the four-fold plan has only been outlined, you are not ready for the next step.

After you have drawn your checker, look at it well. Photograph it on your brain. There you have the picture of the Magic Square—the symbol of the richer, fuller life, the emblem you are to follow in your daring crusade.

The chapters that follow give a definite program for the daring few who are determined to tap all of their inner resources. If you don't feel the urge to Dare don't waste your time to go on. If you lack courage or faith the following pages will not help you. But if you are able and willing to do and dare then immediately assume the offensive.

The day of defending your present possessions is gone. From now on you are not going to worry about holding your job. Put the worry on the fellow above you about holding his. From this day onward wrong things are put on the defense. You have marshalled right things for the attack. Your eyes are turned toward your strength, not your weakness. Henceforth you will wake in the morning thinking of ways to do things, rather than reasons why they can't be done. When Henry Ford wanted to get an unbreakable glass for his new models he wouldn't see any of the experts. They knew too many reasons why it couldn't be done. "Bring me eager young fellows who do not know the reasons why unbreakable glass cannot be made. Give this problem to ambitious young fellows who think nothing is impossible." He got unbreakable glass.

> "That tower of strength
> Which stood four-square to all
> Winds that blew."
> —*Tennyson*

I DARE YOU TO BE STRONG

I often wonder what would have happened to me
if my old school teacher, George Warren Krall,
hadn't dared me to be the healthiest boy in my class.
Certainly I would not have dared what I have tried
to accomplish. Sickness robs us of time, courage
and money. Wealth can't buy health but health can
buy wealth.

Many a young man, today, starting out on a road
he hopes will lead to success, looks at men of affairs
who have gone before him and tries to select those
attributes which will lead him into that charmed
circle of successful men. He will find, however,
it is pretty difficult to determine just what are the
essentials of a successful career. Some leaders are
tall men, some are short men, some are men from
the country, some from the city. Some are men with
college background, others are men whose only
schooling was "reading, 'riting and 'rithmetic."
Some are geniuses, some are pluggers. In an issue
of Fortune, I read an article that gives a brief word
picture of a dozen or more of the leading executives
of the General Motors Corporation. Each man is a
distinct personality—no two came from the same
environment, but I did find one common attribute
of every single one of them. That is *energy*. I think

if you look for the propelling force of any successful executive, you will find it is energy. True, you may find an occasional man who has succeeded in spite of the lack of energy, but for every one of such you will find twenty or thirty have succeeded because of it.

Every time I met Walter Pitkin he fired at me questions such as these:

1) Have I a capacity for hard work?
2) Can I keep everlastingly at it?
3) Have I sustained "Pep and Punch"?
4) Do I maintain a high batting average?
5) What is my ability to spurt?

These are questions that stir me to the depths. How can you maintain energy without health? In our own company, every employee in both office and field must pass a physical examination before he can come on our payroll. Afterwards he must pass a rigid physical examination once a year. Why? Because a fit employee does things. He's worth more than an unfit one.

I like the way Huxley expresses this game of life. ". . . It is very plain that the life, the fortune and the happiness of everyone of us do depend upon our knowing something of the rules of a game infinitely more difficult and complicated than chess. It is a game which has been played for untold ages, every man and woman of us being one of the two players in a game of his or her own. The chessboard is the world, the pieces are the phenomena of the universe, the rules of the game are what we call the laws of nature. The player on the other side is hidden from us. We know that his play is always fair, just and patient. But also we know to our cost, that he never overlooks a mistake or makes the smallest allowance for ignorance. To the man who plays well the highest stakes are paid with that sort of overflowing generosity with which the strong show delight in strength. And one who plays ill is checkmated—without haste but without remorse."

If you were trying to make the football team this fall or the basketball team next winter, would you object to eating at the training table, getting regular sleep and going through the rigorous but stimulating body-building program that would make you fit when the crucial test came? Every day is a crucial test in the game of life. The longer you live the better will you understand that fact. Every time you take liberties with your physical strength, such as eating or drinking things that do not agree with you, or losing sleep, you will find that some day you will pay the price when you need the ability to spurt or maintain a high batting average or need strength for that extra pep and punch when all those around you are weakening.

Life is a bigger game than football or basketball, but the same rules maintain. If you keep strong, physically fit, full of energy and enthusiasm, you are the man whom life's coach is going to pick when the winning touchdown is needed. But if you do not follow the rules, if you become indifferent in the care of your physical strength, then the coach will yank you out of the game and put a more capable person in your place.

Health is the foundation for individual success. Health is one of the greatest assets industry looks for, and health is the foundation of a nation's progress. In 1877, in one of his memorable statements, Disraeli declared that "the health of the people is really the foundation upon which all their happiness and all their power as a state depend. It is quite possible for a kingdom to be inhabited by an able and active population; you may have successful manufacturers and you may have a productive agriculture; the arts may flourish, architecture may cover your land with temples and palaces, you may have even material powers to defend and support all these acquisitions, you may have arms of precision, fleets of warships, but if the population of the country is stationary or yearly diminishing—if, while it diminishes in number it diminishes also in stature, in strength, that country is doomed. The health of the people is, in my opinion, the first duty of a statesman."

As I write this chapter the world is passing through an economic depression. Everybody is being called upon to bear extra burdens. There is a crisis in every nation, in every business, in every household. Woe to the nation or business or individual who has no health reserves! Nerves snap, tempers explode, bodies and minds give way under the strain unless they can call up physical reinforcements. How fortunate the nation, business or individual which has a sturdy constitution capable of shouldering the extra load without faltering.

When leaders command, bodies obey. "Body, what can you do with flabby muscles and faulty digestion? How can you arrive anywhere if you get tired and your energy peters out? That hollow chest and those drooping shoulders will never get you to the top of the ladder. About face! Muscles strong! Chest up! Head erect!" It is difficult at first, but soon the sheer joy of vigorous health amply rewards you for daring to be strong and well.

Sadly enough, it is oftentimes necessary for us to lose our health before we appreciate it. Youth, for instance, is a spendthrift of health and strength because there is such a surplus. It isn't taken seriously. But I am daring you crusaders to take health seriously. I have seen ambitious young men right on the threshold of a striking success crack because of ill health. That's too heavy a price to pay for the privilege of being a spendthrift of health and energy. Why not stay on Mount Health? It is a laborious climb back after you have fallen down the side. Besides, a ride in the ambulance below isn't the most pleasant thing.

One of Technology's most prominent graduates, addressing a small group of students, talked almost solely on the necessity of safeguarding health. He stressed health so strongly, he said, because of his personal acquaintance with so many men whose success had been snatched away because of physical failure just when they were about to reap the reward of a long struggle.

Keeping fit is not a tedious job. Treating your body with the ordinary care you give your automobile or your dog is not a nuisance. Giving your body the stimulation of good, wholesome food is more fun than doping it with artificial stimulants. Again I challenge the scoffers who say that living right is not more thrilling than living wrong. You can keep yourself fit and enjoy doing it. Make it a game. Make it the hard thing to do *not* to eat right, *not* to take regular exercises, *not* to get the proper amount of sleep. You can play bridge until midnight, but not every night and feel rested in the morning. Keep caught up on your sleep. Anybody can ride every place in an automobile. My car is a convenience, but I walk my mile a day because I feel the better for it. It's my program.

My physical life has been a happy one. Why shouldn't it be happy? Good health makes happiness. My friends envy me because I have never lost a day at the office on account of illness. Yet the same friends think I am a faddist on health. And I am a faddist! It pays. Good health has been the most profitable, most enjoyable fad I know. Some faddists don't exercise and don't bother with regular hours. Personally, I would rather have my fad than theirs.

There is no secret to good health other than just plain, good common sense. You wouldn't let your automobile go along, week after week, month after month, without the proper mixture of oil and gas and overhauling. Why, under heaven, do you expect your body to carry on without at least the same consideration? You wouldn't keep a dog or a horse cooped up in a stall all day without a chance to stretch its legs. Then why expect to avoid trouble if you treat your own priceless machine in such a manner? Everybody knows these things, but so few do anything about it. I have never been able to understand why people are not willing to pay the small price for good health.

I don't particularly enjoy getting out of bed in the morning and touching the floor twenty times and twisting my liver fifty times and stretching to the heavens for posture. I don't like these exercises any more than I like to shave. But I wouldn't appear at my office with a bristling beard. That would discount me in the eyes of my associates. I don't like exercising and I don't like shaving, but I'm going to do both. A Scotch friend once told me he didn't like the taste of liquor. "Then why drink it?" I asked him. "For the effect," he replied. Just so, I don't particularly like the immediate taste of morning exercises, but I do like the effect. Even my Scotch friend will agree that exercising is a lot more permanent—and cheaper, too.

I dare you to exercise! Keep yourself fit and enjoy the consequences. Attack it in the right attitude. Let me illustrate:

John and George both begin to take exercises. John crawls out of bed in the morning thinking, "Oh, darn, I've got to take those exercises", and he goes unwillingly through them. In a few days or weeks he is fudging, dropping off one and then two. One night he is out late and next morning is so sleepy he satisfies his "conscience" that the extra few minutes' sleep will do him more good than the exercises. Soon a hundred excuses are found for *not* taking those exercises. John stops, feeling half honest and sincere in doing so.

But now consider George. He believes that exercises every morning will make him a better man all day. He thoroughly establishes that thought in his mind. He knows that *not* to take those exercises puts a burden on him for the rest of the day. When the alarm clock rings, two voices whisper in his ear. One says, "Don't take those exercises. What's the use?" The other voice says, "All right, George, now is your opportunity to start the biggest day of the week. Stretch up those arms, because today you must grow more than yesterday. Squeeze that liver. Get your blood in circulation. A strong body is necessary if you are to tackle that bigger job." Which voice is he going to heed? Then when he, like John, is out late at night, morning finds him with this attitude: "Not so much sleep as usual last night. Brain a bit slower. All the more need for physical strength to meet the opportunities which may come my way. Up and at my exercises. No slipping for me." Which voice are *you* going to heed?

I have a young friend who smoked too much and who refused to take daily exercises. "I hate standing over myself like a policeman," he told me, "always telling myself I must not do this or I must do that. I don't believe it would do me any good to cut out smoking, that is, if I had to threaten myself with a club. To drive myself to exercise every

morning might build me up physically, but it would
certainly wear me down mentally. I like to do the
things I enjoy doing."

Perfectly right, too. Most people do. But I suggested he should *make* himself enjoy doing the
things he did *not* like to do. That sounded like a
paradox and he laughed at me, but soon after his
doctor showed him how it could be done. He became
dangerously ill and the doctor who pulled him
through the critical stage said, "Now go ahead and
smoke all you want, but when you light a cigarette,
just say to yourself, 'This will make it harder for
me to get back my full strength,' and when you get
up in the morning say, 'I won't take any exercise
and I'll soon be back in bed.' " Pretty shrewd judge
of human nature, that doctor. He knew his patient
only did the things he enjoyed doing. He made it
hard to enjoy wrong things and easy to enjoy right
things. Habits rule most of our actions, but they are
mostly mental, and a changed mental attitude can
change a bad habit to a good one.

Long ago I discovered a daily prescription that
agreed with me. The old bootmaker, mentioned by
Hinsdale in his essay, "Atmospheric Air in Relation
to Tuberculosis", has this to say about walking:

> "The best medicine! Two miles of oxygen three
> times a day. This is not only the best, but cheap
> and pleasant to take. It suits all ages and consti-
> tutions. It is patented by infinite wisdom, sealed
> with a signet divine. It cures cold feet, hot heads,
> pale faces, feeble lungs, and bad tempers. If two
> or three take it together, it has a still more strik-

ing effect. It has often been known to reconcile enemies, settle matrimonial quarrels, and bring reluctant parties to a state of double blessedness. This medicine never fails. Spurious compounds are found in large towns; but get into the country lanes, among green fields, or on the mountain top, and you have it in perfection as prepared in the great laboratory of Nature."

I make it a practice to walk a mile a day. For the same reason, I drink eight glasses of water every day, get seven or eight hours' regular sleep, and generally try to obey the common sense laws of Nature that make me feel better. I obey them, not because I have aches and pains, but because I want tingling blood and wide open eyes and sound sleep and healthy appetite. I go to a doctor twice a year, not because there is anything wrong with me, but to make sure that nothing will be wrong.

If our theory, *that valuable possessions, when shared, multiply,* is sound, how can we use the buoyance of our physical life? That glow of personal health—can it be shared? What one of us doesn't buck up when we come in the presence of a man with head erect, shoulders square, chest up? Does he lose by having good health radiate from every fibre of his being? Not a bit of it. As he helps others, his passion for strength grows.

My friend, Dr. Joel E. Goldthwait, has done marvels in building strong men and women. He, himself, is a living example of his theories. Magnificent of posture—tall, straight, deep of chest, clear of eye, ruddy of cheek—he shares his splendid self with his patients. And into every patient Dr. Goldthwait instills a burning desire to build up others. Inevitably, as we carry the gospel of health to others, the more abundant health we possess ourselves.

Before you go on your next adventure, you will want to map out a pretty definite physical program. Nobody can do this for you. It is entirely up to you whether you succeed or fail on this Physical battlefront. Abundant health is such a luxury! Energy is such an asset in business. Physical strength is the backbone of success and happiness in every walk of life. Now you must prove that you are in earnest and want to grow strong. I know from experience that your most sinister enemy is a desire to put off the fight. Unless you begin your Physical Dare program now, you might as well chuck this book.

I have suggested a few things which have helped me physically during my lifetime. All are simple rules, easy to carry out, and have been the powerful contributing factors to the splendid health which I have always enjoyed. Eight hours' sleep. Open windows. Regular daily exercise, morning and night. Eat the things that agree with me—but not overeat. Walk my mile a day. Open air every noontime and on vacations. Plenty of sunshine. Practice simple rules of posture which make me feel better; besides, the man who walks straight and sits straight, I believe thinks straight. And lastly, I have talked health to our employees, to my family and to everybody I meet. As I told you before, they consider me a faddist but I expect to be urging good health on everybody in sight until the day I die.

Please don't think I am trying to give you a complete program for your physical development. That is for you and your doctor or some other competent person to work out. All I want is to put the thought in your head and the urge in your heart to dare something physically. If you have determined to *beat your best* physically, in the next twelve months, why not ask yourself these questions:

1. Am I in good physical condition now?

2. If not, what am I going to do about it?

3. What weakness will I overcome this year?

   For example: bad posture, hollow chest, overweight, underweight, lack of sleep, bad digestion, constipation, headaches.

4. How?

5. What is my big physical Dare for this year ahead?

6. Will I store up enough surplus energy to carry me through my "Beat My Best" year? I will need strong reserves. Can't afford to weaken in the last round. That's when my enemies falter. Extra energy—extra punch!

7. What will I *definitely* do about this?

8. Will I stick to this Dare until I win out?

I am going to dare to suggest that after answering the above questions on a sheet of paper, you decide on a very definite program. One of my associates who, in one year, made the greatest physical progress of his life, gave me the following sights which turned a defeat into a victory.

SIGHTS	HOW	DID I DO IT?
Eliminate illness of last year.	Have thorough physical examination on my birthday, February 15th, and have every recommendation of the doctor carried out before March 30th.	Examined February 15th. Doctor recommended dental treatment. Done March 10th.
	Eating meat only once a day recommended.	
Taper off and finally cut out smoking for one month.	No smoking during Lent.	Succeeded.
Get more sleep.	Average seven hours a night; better still, eight.	Yes.

Double the amount of fresh air I get.	Sleep with windows open.	Yes.
Correct constipation.	Exercise 10 minutes every morning and evening.	Missed only two days.
Correct stooped shoulders.	Put a sign "Don't buckle at the waist" on my desk. Practice "abdomen in, hips flat, chest up, chin in" at least five times each day by standing back against a wall—hips, shoulders, head, all touching the wall.	Yes. December 3rd.
Have regular walking program.	Walk a mile every day. Don't say you haven't time. Do it.	Yes.
Balance my diet.	Read book on Diet and Health and profit by it.	OK.
	Eat some good wholesome cereal every day.	Yes.
	Eat meat only once a day and a green salad every day.	Yes.

Cut down weight five pounds.	Cut out desserts at noon.	Yes.

In order to make you posture-conscious, I want to add a few illustrations and suggest three simple exercises.*

When a man takes a chair in my office and slides down on his backbone, I feel like yanking him up by the back of the neck.

When a man sits straight I believe he can think straight.

*Taken from Mr. Danforth's book "Growth."

When I pass a man with head erect, chin in, shoulders square, abdomen in, he is such an inspiration to me that I straighten up, too. Straighten Up!

When a girl sits opposite me at meal time with shoulders slouched down and all buckled up at the waist, I can hardly keep from saying, "Straighten up!"

*Johnny has good
posture

*Susie has poor
posture

*Illustrations from Hygeia.

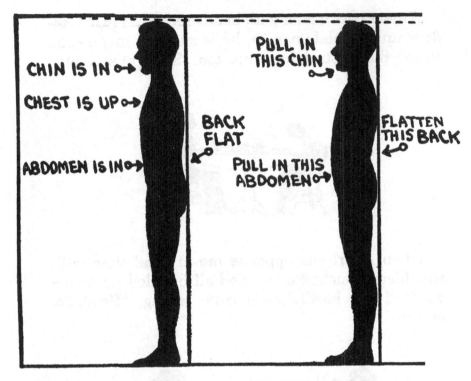

(A) The "Stand Tall" Posture
This is the aristocratic bearing.
You *know* this man is happy
and successful.

(B) The "Watch Out" Posture
This posture is still good but slipping. It probably belongs to **one**
who has always stood tall, but **has**
now begun to take things easy.

In which of these four classes do you belong?
Certainly you can't afford to guess: because most of
us think our posture is better than it really is. After
you take your bath tomorrow morning, stand in
front of a full length mirror or place a light so that it
casts your shadow on a white wall. Get your wife or

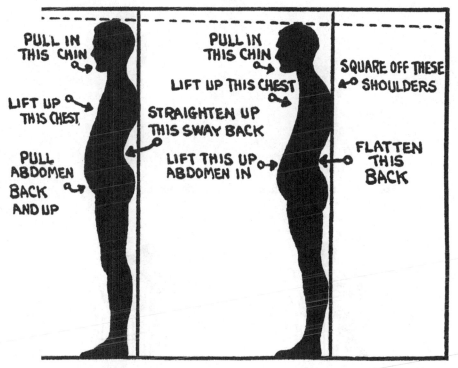

PULL IN
THIS CHIN

LIFT UP
THIS CHEST

PULL
ABDOMEN
BACK
AND UP

PULL IN
THIS CHIN

LIFT UP THIS CHEST

STRAIGHTEN UP
THIS SWAY BACK

LIFT THIS UP
ABDOMEN IN

SQUARE OFF THESE
SHOULDERS

FLATTEN
THIS
BACK

(C) The "Trouble Ahead" Posture
this belongs to the person who
never remembers to stand or sit
straight. He slumps at the desk,
crouches when he walks and curls
to in an easy chair in the evening.

(D) The "Trouble Is Here" Posture
This person has gone so long without
straightening up that there is a complete let-down in his muscles. He has
indigestion, constipation, rheumatism
and goodness knows what not.

roommate to take the four figures shown above and
tell you in which one you belong. Mark your height
on a wall because you will notice in the above figures
that good posture makes you taller. If you improve
your posture you will actually "Grow" in stature.
What could be more fitting for a growth year than
to increase your height?

Stand tall at your office

The wrong way to stand

Sit at attention

The wrong way to sit

Which one of these girls is the happy, healthy one?
Remember—backbone straight

Here's another test. Stand up straight to a wall with toes touching. If your posture is correct the wall will just touch your chest but no other part of your body and it will miss your nose about an inch. Mark your height on the wall.

Three Simple Daily Posture Exercises

Don't expect to jump a class in posture overnight. It took several years to "get" your present posture, allow at least a few months to show improvement. Remember, posture is largely a matter of mind. If you can remember to straighten up, you will. In order to help you remember, try these three simple exercises every day:

1. *Abdomen In*

Before you get out of bed in the morning, pull the pillow from under your head, lie flat on your back, put both hands on back of neck and pull in your abdomen. Try to pull all of your intestines up under your ribs. Do this ten times. Do it ten more times before going to sleep at night.

HANDS CLASPED
UNDER HEAD   PULL IN HERE

2. *Stand Tall*

Jump out of bed, put both
hands on top of your head
and stretch yourself up as
high as you can, hold it a
second, then relax. Repeat
this ten times. Then again
at night before going to
bed.

3. *Walk at Attention*

The first block that you walk after leaving your
house, to the street car, pull yourself to attention—
chin in, chest up, abdomen in—and walk as though
you were passing General Pershing in a reviewing

stand. "Push out your third vest
button." Next week do it two
blocks. If you drive to work,
take a walk at noon "at attention". After a while you will
get the habit of straightening up
whenever you start to walk.
You will find too that walking
straight makes you feel like
"cutting loose" at a brisk pace
with arms swinging—all of
which means more air in the
lungs, better blood circulation
and better health.

I DARE YOU TO THINK CREATIVELY

Look here, Mind, you can't command **unless** you first learn to obey. You can't direct others without training. K. P. minds stay in the kitchen. The mind of a General makes one a General. Victories are thought out before they are fought out on the battlefield. What do you mean, Mind, by thinking on a low plane when I am daring to set High Achievement as my goal?

In "Pygmalion", Bernard Shaw's professor declares he can take a flower girl of the slums and make her into a real lady. "Think like a duchess, act like a duchess, talk like a duchess—curbstone English keeps you in the gutter," he says to her. When you try to put such thoughts as these in your mind, if it is like the average mind, I can hear it reply, "Don't bother me. I haven't time for these things. I've got enough to think about now. I'll get along all right."

"What's that?" I can hear you answer, "You haven't time for these things?" "Nonsense. You've as much time as anybody. You'd better get Arnold Bennett's little book, 'How to Live on Twenty-four Hours a Day.' It will open up possibilities to you, and it costs less than a dollar. You'll get along all right, will you? Well, how about your study pro-

gram? You haven't time to do any more studying?
You mean the real truth is that you haven't time to
do other things."

So the average mind answers back. Daring people
can't afford not to think. Just as you can't afford
not to exercise. The big prizes are for those who
dare to think hard, to think often, to think creatively. I've spent a lifetime in business, but never
before have I seen such a demand for ideas. Ideas
have always been the dynamos that move civiliza-
tion forward. Stephenson had an idea of a loco-
motive long before rails were laid—but it took years
and years before his idea was accepted. Today, ideas
get an audience immediately. Industry is at the feet
of creative thinkers begging for ideas.

Not many years ago a professor at Oberlin College
suggested to his class that some day a new metal
called aluminum would be economically produced
so that it could be used for a thousand practical
purposes. He said, "It has never been set free. A
fortune awaits the man who can release aluminum."
That word fell as seed into the mind of Charles Hall,
a young boy less than twenty years of age. He was
the son of a missionary to the West Indies. He began
to work with little crucibles furnished by the professor and finally showed him a drop of pure aluminum and then dared to set out to discover aluminum
in commerical quantities. He did, and when he died
he left one-third of his immense aluminum fortune
to Oberlin College, one-third to Foreign Missions;
the other third he left to Berea College and the
American Missionary Association. Oberlin gave an

idea and a dare to Charles Hall, and he gave back to Oberlin a rich dividend. The whole world benefited when Charles Hall dared to think creatively along uncharted fields.

Most of the unexplored regions of the world may have been discovered, but what a field lies ahead for the mental Columbus, the thinking Peary, the planning Byrd. Physical adventure promises not half the thrill of mental adventure. Physical life brings happiness, but mental life brings interest—a consuming, absorbing interest. How I pity that person, young or old, who cannot shut out the world, open a book, and go forth on an adventure of romance, travel, biography, history or business. What a shame to see so many mental lives slow down after school days are over, just because people forget the necessity of everlastingly studying if they expect to get anywhere. Theodore Roosevelt died with a book under his pillow; consuming the ideas of others until the very last. Have you read Abbé Dimnet's "The Art of Thinking"? If not, buy it right away. Don't get it from the library. Own it. Lose no time. Its pages fascinatingly lead you into a new mental realm. If you already have a copy, dust it off and read it over again. Stagnant minds are the greatest obstacles to progress.

I spent an afternoon with Charles F. Kettering, President of the General Motors Research Corporation, and one of the keenest creative minds in America. After he moved to the city and "became famous", so the story goes, his mother still lived on the old home place in the country and burned coal-oil lamps. Why shouldn't she have bright lights just as he had in the city? He must see to it. He did. Result—the Delco system which illumines the farm houses of our country. Mr. Kettering got tired of jumping out of his car and cranking it up. Why not start the car from a switch on the dashboard? Off went the creative mind on another excursion—the self-starter was the result. He found that it took 31 days to paint an auto—one coat on another with the proper time for drying. The paint men got their heads together, they thought that one day or possibly two at the outside might be saved. Kettering said he wanted it done in *one hour*. He was crazy! But a way was found. On some toys, a quick drying enamel was used. It wouldn't do for autos. Why? "It dries too damn fast." When he would spray it, he found that it would dry before it reached the *surface*. He kept on until Duco was produced and an auto was painted complete *in an hour*.

On one occasion Mr. Kettering brought a group of automobile manufacturers into a conference. He told them to write down all the improvements they would want for the next four years and leave their slips of paper on his desk. Then he took them through his research laboratory, showing them what was in progress. Coming back, one man reached for his paper and tore it up. "Hey, there, what do you mean?" said Mr. Kettering. "We only asked for little five-cent improvement. We didn't know how to ask for enough. You are years and years ahead of us," was the reply.

In St. Louis we had an outstanding brain surgeon who was head of our Washington University brain surgery clinic. His operations were almost miraculous. Cases were brought to him from thousands of miles away. "Lucky beggar", says the young medical student, "to be born with such skill." But wait a minute, let us look at Dr. Ernest Sachs' history.

A number of years ago, when he was an intern in a New York hospital, one of his chiefs bemoaned the fact that the majority of brain tumors were fatal. He prophesied that some day some surgeon would dare to find out how to save these lives. Young Ernest Sachs dared to be that surgeon. He dared to face an almost hopeless task. There was no background of successful brain surgery in America at that time. The only possible guidepost the young adventurer could steer for was a doctor in England, Sir Victor Horsley, who knew more about the anatomy of the brain than any other living man. He was the pioneer in brain surgery in England. Dr. Sachs received permission to study under this English scientist. But here is an interesting thing that he did before studying in England.

In order to become rooted and grounded in the knowledge and technique that he should possess before working under this eminent surgeon, he spent six months studying in Germany under the most able men there. Not many young students would be willing to do that. The English doctor was so impressed with the earnestness and industry of the young American who would spend six months in pre-preparation that he brought him right into his home. Together during two years they worked out long and intricate experiments on many dozens of monkeys. Thus the basic facts were found and the background laid for Dr. Sachs' future career.

He returned to America and here was laughed at when he asked for the opportunity to treat brain tumors. For years he fought discouragements and obstacles. He worked without facilities, but with that unconquerable urge that gets things done. Today the majority of brain tumors can be cured. Today Dr. Sachs shares his gifts by the training of young doctors and establishing them in different centers of this country so that each section may have a brain surgeon nearer home. His book, "The Diagnosis and Treatment of Brain Tumors" has been adopted the standard authority on this baffling subject.

Tong-g-g-g-g-g! A Serbian shepherd boy struck the handle of a long knife. The blade was buried in the ground of the pasture field so the signal did not reach the marauders hiding in the long corn nearby. But it did reach other shepherd boys scattered across the field, each with an ear pressed tight against the ground. By means of this ingenious system of sending signals through the ground the Serbian shepherd boys outwitted the Roumanian cattle thieves who crept up under cover of darkness and the tall corn.

All except one of those shepherd boys grew up and forgot all about the phenomenon of the ground signals. But one boy remembered and twenty-five years later applied the principle with the result that

he made one of the greatest inventions of the age.
So Michael Pupin, that humble shepherd boy,
changed the telephone from a device that could be
used to speak only across a city to a long distance
instrument that could be heard across a continent.

The Edisons and the Marconis were the long
range thinkers of yesterday. Wanted—some long
range thinkers today! Where yesterday a hundred
new inventions were made, a thousand new ones
will be made tomorrow and some of you who read
this message will dare to make them. I read an
article not long ago where somebody prophesied
conditions twenty years from now. Our homes
would be artificially cooled in the summer just as
they are artificially heated in the winter. Trans-
portation will be just as different from today as today is from the gay '90's. People will dress differently, think differently, live differently. Are you
leaders going to sit back and wait for yourselves to
be adapted to these conditions? Or, are you going
to be one of those who help bring about these
changes?

"I have no opportunity to create," you say. No
opportunity? Bosh! Opportunities to create are
popping out at you every minute of the day. Some
of the greatest creations have come from minds
able to interpret the usual in an unusual way.

Once a professor hit upon a great discovery while
buttoning up his vest. Or rather, he hit upon the
discovery because his vest wouldn't button up. His
little daughter had sewn up some of the button-
holes. His fingers were going along as usual in

their most intricate operations of buttoning a button. If you want to know how intricate these operations are, you might try it yourself. Just try con-
sciously buttoning up one button. But be sure and
count each thing that each thumb and finger does.
Each move that they make. Then you will be able
to start on this story where the professor started.

His buttoning was going on in the usual way,
when something happened. A button wouldn't
button.

The fingers fumbled helplessly for a moment,
then sent out a call for help. The mind woke up.
The eyes looked down . . . a new idea was born, or
rather a new understanding of an old idea. What
the professor had discovered was that fingers can
remember. They call it physiological memory now.

Then he began playing pranks on his classes, and
he found that the answer was always the same. As
long as they could keep on doing the things they
had always done, their minds wouldn't work. It
was only when he figuratively sewed up their
button-holes, stole their notebooks, upset their
routine, threatened them with failure, that any
thinking was done.

So he came to the great, and now generally accepted, conclusion that the mind of man is "an
emergency organ," that it relegates everything possible to other functions of the body as long as it is
able, that it is only when the old order of things
won't work any longer that it gets on the job.

I am indebted to an advertisement in the New
York Times for the above on a man buttoning up

his vest.   But history is full of such commonplaces that turn our minds topsy-turvy.

One day in Denmark, Dr. Finsen stood gazing absent-mindedly out of his window.   A cat lay dozing in the sun.   The shadows lengthened and slowly shut off the sun from the cat. Tabby awoke, got up and went farther into the sun.   Again the shadows crept up and again the cat moved into the sunlight. Finsen's curiosity was aroused.   What made the cat stay in the sun?   If light and heat are good for a cat, wouldn't they be good for people?   And that was the starting point of his world-famous light-cure work.

Igo Etrich, the inventor of the Taube flying machine, got his idea in India from the seed of the zanonia.   The turned-up wing tips of this natural "plane" became the principle of the war-famous German fighting plane.

Dr. Holmes, a noted psychologist, says that 95% of people think an aimless, desultory, gossipy flow of ideas and only 5% aim definitely direct, and definitely arrive at conclusions.

You daring adventurers in the mental realms— you can't all be Halls, Ketterings, Sachs, Pupins or Finsens, but you are not afraid to tackle the impossible, are you?   "It can't be done" is a finality to those afraid to dare.   But you crusaders are looking for things which can't be done.   All the easy things have been done long ago.   Now bring on the impossible!

Your mental program and the development of your mental self you must work out for yourself,

but let me give you some of the few things that I
have found very valuable in my own life. I am
pretty much of the opinion that nobody was born a
genius. I am coming more and more to Carlyle's
definition of genius—"an infinite capacity for hard
work." You have heard this over and over again,
but have you benefited by it?

The other day one of our sales managers was
talking about one of the brilliant young salesmen
whom he employed a year before, who seemed to
have the personality, the appearance and ability to
go a long way. But he didn't, and the sales man-
ager, after having fired him, told me that the man
was just "plain dumb." He knew a little bit about
everything, but when he got right down into a
discussion of specific things, he just wasn't there.
Only froth on top. I recall the flying fish I saw in
the Indian Ocean. They flash up in the air for a
minute, flutter and scintillate in the sun and then
fall back into the sea. Who wants to be a flying
fish, shining for a minute and then sinking out of
sight? When it is so easy to get our thinking done
for us, the big temptation is not to think. We
glance at the newspaper headlines and let them
form our opinions, and neglect to read the scholarly
articles in the monthly magazine that would give
us the meat on the subject. We listen to a few
minutes of the radio and flatter ourselves that we
know all about the Symphony. We read a review
of a play and decide that we don't need to see the
play itself. These are the temptations of the
average person today, but if you have read this far,

I assume that you are above the average person. I am daring you to know at least one thing well. What is it? Make your decision and then determine to know that one thing well, better than anyone else. In doing this you will have to think. No one is going to get far these days unless he thinks for himself. This is going to take time and hard work, but the joy you will discover in knowing one thing well will more than repay you.

I remember a story they used to tell about old Bill Brown down in my section of the country. He used to plow the field in the spring with a yoke of oxen. He would holler "Gee" and "Haw" at them, but they paid no attention to him. "Then go any way you durn please," said Bill, "the whole field has got to be plowed anyway." No crusader can turn his mental powers loose. Life has to be lived, the field has to be plowed, but it's the way you live it and the way you plow that count in the long run. You are alert. How dare you let mental oxen lead you around the field? You are the crusaders who are going to do things. You must plow a better furrow than ever has been plowed, even if it is only one furrow. You must harvest a better crop than ever has been harvested, even if it is only a few bushels. You recognize the danger as well as the disgrace of a half-used mind. You are going to gear up your mind to capacity and share its strength with others. Instead of diminishing by sharing, you will grow increasingly strong.

Train for the fight. Fit yourself for larger responsibility by studying outside of regular hours.

Reading the right kinds of books improves your background and stimulates your brain. This minute, why not write down the name of one particular book you can't afford *not* to read........? You know where you are headed. Then do some more exploring in that field through books. I'd like to recommend my rule of thumb for a minimum program—"I'll read one book a month." I use the last blank page of a book to make suggestive notes so that I can in the future catch at a glance the high points of the book which may be of personal profit to me.

You have to train for your mental crusade just as you train for your physical game of life. You can do that in the same time you spend on the comic page in the daily paper. It will benefit you a lot more.

I have always loved good books. Titles, as well as contents, start me on new adventures. The first book I can remember was called "Purpose." I don't know who wrote it. My mother gave it to me when I was a slip of a boy. Its very name went deep into my life. In later years I read "The Charm of the Impossible" by Margaret Slattery and "The Lure of the Labrador Wild" by Dillon Wallace—thrilling titles that stir the soul and make you want to do something. Then "One Increasing Purpose," "So Big," "Giants in the Earth," "The Quest of the Best," "He Can Who Thinks He Can," "Magnificent Obsession," "Men of Iron." How these titles gripped me. "The Psychology of Achievement" by Pitkin, and "The Marks of an Educated Man" by

Wiggam, are among my favorites. Some critics may laugh at this, but somehow titles as well as contents seem to put a dare into me.

"He has the notebook habit," I heard a man say. Well, that's one of my mental habits which has proven very valuable in more ways than one. It is all right to develop your memory but I have found a notebook a most valuable memory aid. I always carry one in my inside coat pocket. I even keep one close beside my bed and many a time in the middle of the night I have jotted down something that I could never have recalled had I not had a pencil and paper handy.

Speaking of habits, how about some other old habit that is making a fool of you right before your eyes? The thing to do is to turn the whole procedure around and make a fool of that old habit. It is really a ridiculous situation that a mind of inherent strength cannot have its own way and master any habit.

One of our advertising men, Mr. Brandon, told me he had been smoking so many cigarettes the habit was making a fool of him—robbing him of his physical reserves. So, he decided to make a fool out of that habit. And here's the way he turned the tables:

He knew if he went around feeling sorry for himself because he couldn't smoke, he was sunk. It was all right to say "exert his will power," but that made his temper short and his work suffer. He decided the thing to do was to get a new habit immediately to replace smoking. A habit he could use to replace the habit of smoking.

Now, he says, when we see him standing in front of an open window taking deep breaths, he is smoking. When he disinfects his throat with a gargle, he is smoking. When he is brushing his teeth directly after eating, he is smoking. In that way he formed new habits that have taken the place of the old smoking one.

John was a great dreamer. He built castles in the air a mile high—and left them in the air.

Bill was also a dreamer. He, too, built his air castles. But he had the faculty of bringing those castles down to earth. He would pile them in front of him. Then he would attack them—and counter-attack them. He was as merciless in his cross examination as any officer giving a criminal the third degree. Dreams that were wild he pulled out of the pile as he would pull a wet faggot out of the fire. But of those other dreams—the worthwhile ones, he demanded action. He *ordered* them to come true. Yes, Bill was a dreamer, but in addition he had that rare executive ability that tested, selected, then *made* his dreams come true.

Try Bill's methods. You have dreams. They will come true—I ask you *when?*

Most of us would like to be a Bernard Shaw or a Thomas A. Edison today. But how many would have been willing to be a Shaw or an Edison fifty years ago when they were constantly laboring, studying, training, and devouring all they could

find which would fit them for the fame that was to
be theirs?   Ask your author friends if each book
doesn't represent months, even years of hard labor.
No man can give out unless he first takes in.   You
can't give what you don't have.   Let me give you a
challenge, a definite mental challenge.   For one
solid month, dare to think fearlessly in some one
uncharted field.   When you read a book don't let
the author do all of your thinking for you.   Stop at
the end of that sentence, or page, or chapter which
brings you up with a start.   Interpret these thoughts
into something definite in your own life.   How can
you apply it in your work tomorrow?   Venture
courageously into new mental realms.   Think orig-
inally.   If you can contribute one ounce of original
thought, if you can originate just one new idea,
you have dared well.   This is to be your mental
offensive campaign.   Let's become sick and tired
of being always on the defensive.

Finally, don't you dare stop until you have produced at least one creative idea.   One creative mind
dared to put the hind end of a needle on the point
—a little thing, but out of it came the sewing
machine.   The Hindenburg line wasn't crossed
easily.   You'll have to adventure in No Man's Land
and dig in many times before you reach your
objective.   The Allied Armies paid the price, but
they smashed through.   I dare you, I double dare
you, to be a Creator—a Hunger Fighter, a Microbe
Hunter.   Make a start!   Never stop until you can put
down in black and white some one idea or thing
that you have created.

May I add one word about the subconscious mind? As a business man, I don't know one thing about it, but I'm going to learn. If I can set my subconscious mind like an alarm clock before I go to bed at night, then wake up in the morning brimful of ideas, I'll keep in the Daring class. Better have a program to include the subconscious.

Perhaps what I have said here sounds too big and mighty to be accomplished. "I am not a genius. I haven't the capacity to be a Hunger Fighter, or a great scientist, or an author." Well, let's not think what you cannot do. What interests me is what you *can do*. Are you satisfied with what your mind has accomplished so far? Has it done the best it is capable of? I'll warrant it has not. Then your job is to know how much more mental ability you have, then *dare* to use it.

Remember that *valuable possessions multiply when shared*. Your mind begins to grow as you share it. How much more enjoyable is a book when you discuss it or maybe lend or pass it to friends with certain passages marked. You are a multiplier when you clip a good idea from the morning paper and pass it along to that person who is particularly interested. Telling an unusual story to others helps you fix it in your mind. How much more clearly a problem crystallizes in our mind when we present it to another. You give a big idea to your friend. He gives a big idea to you. You both have two ideas. Sharing increases.

Alas, there are some who will agree to all this and say, "That's good stuff," then never *do* a blessed thing. Or, they will try just one thing then another but they will do them in a half-hearted way. They will never get anywhere. But you Crusaders, you are going to do these things. You are alert. You recognize the danger as well as the disgrace of a half-used mind. You are going to gear up your mind to capacity and share its strength with others. Instead of diminishing by sharing, you will grow increasingly strong.

Outline on a sheet of paper the following or a similar program for your Mental Dare. The weak ones who are licked or partially licked will stall here. Will you listen to the little imps whispering in your ears that writing down the things you ought to do is merely piffle? Or will you put things down in black and white that need to be done and never quit until you can say "Done!"?

MY MENTAL DARES	MY MENTAL ACCOMPLISHMENTS
1. One Habit to about-face	1. When conquered
2. One Idea to Create	2. Creative Development
3. One month's thinking in uncharted fields	3. Results obtained

4. My program is growing   4. What progress?
   by sharing

5. What is my biggest   5. Daringly done
   Mental Dare for the
   year ahead?

I DARE YOU TO DEVELOP A
MAGNETIC PERSONALITY

If you were applying to us for a position in our business, I would first ask the doctor to report on your physical condition. I would want to be sure that you were well and had the stamina and strength to finish any program you would start. Then I would have the Personnel Department check your mental capacity and background. After being satisfied that you are physically and mentally fit, do you think that is all I want to know about you? Not by long odds. I want to see you and talk to you. But why? Isn't all the information we need to know on these reports? No, there is something more I must know, something that can't easily be put down on paper.

You walk into my office. I may notice the cut of your clothes, the way you comb your hair, your shoes, your nails, any stains on your fingers—we always give each other the "once over," don't we? But the big thing is, have you got that something called Personality. It may be akin to that "It" which I used to hear our young people talk about. I am looking for that indescribable quality which attracts people to you. If you give me a flabby handshake, if you have a grouchy look with

the corners of your mouth turned down—we don't
want you around.   Faces that smile, voices that
ring, steps that are firm, interests that are broad—
likeable personalities.   These are the things that
attract business and the whole world, too, for that
matter.   Obstacles just melt away before the sunshine of a smile.   Such leaders with the ability to
make friends can dare twice as much as the lone
wolf.

What is this Personality?   Is it "That Something" born in some people and not in others?   Can
it be developed?   Of course it can.   Undoubtedly
some people are blest with a greater capacity for
this social side than others.   Because Bill has more
personality than I have doesn't mean that I shouldn't
develop mine.   Many a country boy has joined our
sales force and been almost too timid to interview
prospective consumers.   But I have seen these same
boys in a few years so develop and broaden their
personalities that they now stand on a platform
before hundreds of people and speak with confidence, poise, and power.   These boys attract their
audiences, not by memorizing their speeches, but
by finding out a community's needs and with the
fervor of an evangelist by supplying those needs.
Service is a much overused word, but the development of real service is the enlargement of personality.

"But what am I to dare in the social side?" you
ask.   Shall I be a social lion?   Not exactly.   Perhaps
your particular dare is *not* to be a social lion.   If
dancing, bridge and clubs take more than their

share of time from the other three sides of your checker, I dare you to give them their proper place. Perhaps here is an idea that will help you develop that magnetic personality so essential to the complete life.

In the daily paper you read of some great man who has passed on. Who will dare to fill his shoes? Think of all the friends he has left behind, his influence in business and education. He has been an uplifting power in the community. Paying his bills and fulfilling his lawful obligations have been the smallest parts of his life. What was his personality? What particular things about him inspired his associates and drew people to him? Having discovered what the world has lost through the absence of this personality, why not dare to put it back into the living again? Live as that man lived. Think as he would think. Try to fill his place. As a young man I met John Wanamaker. His fine ideals and business ability deeply impressed me. Later when a problem came up that needed sound judgment, I would say, "How would John Wanamaker decide?" This program of trying to fill the shoes of a great man who has gone on may stagger you. You haven't the stuff in you to give. But you have something. Make a start. Give what you have. Every little bit that you give increases your personality by much more than you give.

Personality is a vague, intangible thing to talk about on paper. But how real, how tremendous it is in life all around us! I like the way Miss Helen Gill Lovett described personality. During her active teaching years, she was on our American Youth Foundation Summer Camp Staff and used the different sources of water at the Camps to illustrate four different kinds of personality.

The first is like a mountain stream at the New Hampshire Camp. It sings as it tumbles down the hills into the lake and wherever we touch it there is a supply of fresh pure water. Some personalities are like that. Whether you meet them on the mountain top or down at the lake, they are always sparkling, always singing. Their presence chases gloom and inspires us to go joyfully along with them. Where they lead, all follow; when they smile, all smile; and they are always ready to stimulate us and quench our thirst by sharing with us all they have.

P. G. ("Plug") Orwig, the Director of the American Youth Foundation, is a mountain stream personality. His Indian name is "Wadjepi," the nimble one. If you meet him in camp or on a duck hunt or on the street, or in his home, I dare you to go away depressed. "Wadjepi" gives everybody he meets a refreshing smile, an infectious laugh, a mental pat on the back. He wasn't born with all this capacity. He developed it by giving it away. When he sees someone with the "blues" he turns on the sunshine. I like to be around "Wadjepi."

Down by the lake into which the mountain stream tumbles is a spring. It illustrates the second kind of personality. It is more quiet than the singing mountain stream, but from its bubbling depths comes the coldest, most refreshing drink. The

depth and strength of many quiet lives are a joy
and blessing when shared with others.

"Dad" Waite, former director with P. G. Orwig
in the American Youth Foundation, is the deep
spring personality. He is a comforter, a helper.
"Dad" expresses his personality; because to thousands he is a father, sympathetic, helpful and understanding.

In the Michigan Camp there is an old pump that
squeaks and groans terribly when it works. But
if you have patience and endurance enough to keep
pumping it brings up pure cold water from a deep
well. A few years ago I was on a French diner
eating breakfast on the way to Marseilles where I
was to take sail for India. An Englishman came
in and sat opposite me. He ordered tea. He was
plainly unsociable. The French waiters were slow
bringing his tea, and his ire kept rising. Finally
they brought him a cup of coffee. He drank it
without sugar or cream, growling all the time that
he had ordered tea. They brought him a second
cup of coffee. By that time he was ready to
explode, but he drank it and proceeded to tell all
French waiters what would happen if he did not
get his tea. If I had left the diner at that time I
would have gone away with the conviction that he
was a very disagreeable person. But, fortunately,
his tea arrived and with it his good humor. He
introduced himself to me, discovered we were to
be on the same boat going to India, and later on
was the means of making scores of contacts for me
in the Far East that were unexpected and by far

the most interesting part of my visit there. More than that, we struck up a lasting friendship and I have discovered him to be one of the most interesting personalities I know. Don't always judge a pump by the squeaks it makes, nor a chance acquaintance. Keep on drawing out to find the deeper treasure of rich personality down the well. And vice versa remember that to be cranky and ill-tempered may be over-shadowing your good qualities to such an extent that you are driving friends away from you. The job of your personality is to attract, not to repel.

Close beside the pump is a Memorial Fountain. Built of boulders, strong and imposing, it makes a striking appearance. It is connected to an abundant water supply and through it four bubbling fountains bring cold water to the thirsty. But this past summer there was a new patent connection with the sources of supply and this connection got out of order. The fountain above was beautiful. The water below was pure and bountiful, but just a little something wrong and the fountain was of no practical use. Personality is an illusive thing. Good looks, good habits, good education, fine family, magnificent supply of the best of life to draw from, and yet something lacking in the connections.

I know a girl like that fountain. She had so much to give, but never gave. At present she is a woman soured on life, blaming everybody but herself for her melancholy. In reality, it is her own selfishness to blame. She allowed her personality to get "out-of-order" and she never fixed it.

If you are as I am you will want a few rules that you can get your teeth into. "All of this talk about personality is all right," I can hear you saying, "but what can I do specifically to develop my personality?" The only way I can answer this is from my own practical experience. The first thing that I would do to develop my social side would be to make worthwhile contacts.

When I was a young man, Henry M. Flagler's name was on every tongue. He was treasurer of the Standard Oil Company and a close associate of John D. Rockefeller. Mr. Flagler poured his riches into Florida, building the East Coast Railroad across the Florida Keys and also a chain of hotels. At one time I was in Palm Beach when he was just completing a marble palace for his home. I determined to meet Mr. Flagler. I felt that the inspiration of such a successful man would have a stimulating effect on my whole life. It was easy for me to meet people on my own level, but how was I ever going to meet such a big man as Mr. Flagler? If I didn't meet people who thought bigger, acted bigger and were bigger—much bigger than myself—I argued, how could I ever grow bigger? Here I was in the same town with a man who had become one of the most outstanding successes in America. I had no pull, no introductions, but "fools rush in where angels fear to tread." So I wrote him a frank note telling him that I was a young man full of ambition, just starting in business and that I had a great desire to meet him. To my immense surprise an answer quickly came back inviting me to his home. I feel embarrassed, even now, to think how long I stayed. That day is a highlight in my memory. He showed me his home. I never was in such fairyland before, never knew such splendor existed. We walked around his beautiful gardens. He told me of Mr. Rockefeller and those early beginnings with mountainous obstacles. My mind was filled to saturation. At one time, I remember stopping short and saying, "Mr. Flagler, this is a great privilege to me. Your experiences thrill me. I'm afraid I will forget some of the rules of your life. Do you mind if I write them down in my notebook?" (Even then I had a little book with me and had started the habit of making notes.) "Certainly not," said Mr. Flagler. Then I wrote "Great Responsibility — Great Accountability," and page after page of his rules of life. I feel a glow even now as I think over that rare interview.

The day after I met Mr. Flagler it was impossible for me to act on the same plane as I had acted the day before. Incidentally, that taught me a very vivid lesson: a man who has made a success has a responsibility to those who are striving to make a success. I would like to believe also that the time he gave me in recalling memories helped him to pass along the finer things for which his life stood.

That day, with Mr. Flagler, was a turning point in my life. That chance meeting with the man in the French dining car made my trip to India a rare experience instead of just an ordinary tour. I try to learn something from every great personality with whom I come into contact. If I don't learn something from him I am to blame and I have wasted the time of the greater personality.

For instance, after meeting Ozora S. Davis, formerly of the Chicago Theological Seminary, I said to myself, "What is that rich inspiring something in this man's personality? How can I acquire it so I can inspire others as he has me?" From Sherwood Eddy I have always tried to capture that urge which sends him around the world for a Cause—that "something more" which stirs men to high achievement. When I meet Charles R. Brown I try to absorb some of his magnetic spark so that I, too, might quicken the souls of men around me. And from Dr. Joel E. Goldthwait I try to catch his secret of inspiring men and women to take proper care of their physical selves so as to live gloriously. Yes, I have found it pays to come into contact with great men, but it pays more to try to emulate them.

I read in the New York Journal a fable which illustrates one of the best personality rules which I could give you to develop contacts of all kinds.

"The North Wind and the Sun disputed which was the most powerful, and agreed that he should be declared the victor who could first strip a wayfaring man of his clothes.

"The North Wind first tried his power, and blew with all his might, but the keener became his blasts, the closer the traveler wrapped his cloak around him, till at last, resigning all hope of victory, he called upon the Sun to see what he could do.

"The Sun suddenly shone out with all his warmth. The traveler no sooner felt his genial rays than he took off one garment after another, and at last, fairly overcome with heat, undressed, and bathed in a stream that lay in his path.

"Persuasion is better than force."

I dare you to develop that magnetic personality that will lead and inspire others. You can have that personality if you have a great enough desire. You can become pretty much what you want to be. Can you imagine a young man with a sincere and earnest desire to make friends, ever turning out a grouch? If a young woman really desires to be an interesting conversationalist, she will be one.

When I was a young man I saw the advertisement of a book guaranteeing to develop personal magnetism. It cost me three dollars and I didn't have any three dollars to squander. The book said, "When you enter a room everybody will say, 'Look, there he comes.' " I hadn't read very many pages until I realized that personality is developed from within and that a book only gives you suggestions to work out for yourself. I did get one or two valuable helps which have stayed with me and which I'm going to pass on to you. "Always walk on the sunny side of the street. The warmth and power of the sun enter your system. Its rays give your face a glow and you reflect sunshine to others." With that conscious thought in my mind, I still walk on the sunny side of the street. Then again, "When you wash, put your head down in

the basin, and always wash your face up, not down.
Wash the corners of your mouth up into a smile
and not down into a grouch." Of course, personality depends on more than such superficial things.
But the big thought I got out of it all was, that if
the desire to be sunny and smiling and interesting
was strong enough, then every action such as
walking and washing influenced our personality.

What are the ways to develop personality? They
are simple things and easily overlooked but they
are very vital in the building of this side of a
complete life. In looking back over the men of
great personalities I have known and do know
there are certain common characteristics they all
have. For instance, Mr. Flagler had a broad sym-
pathy. He was able to put himself in my shoes.
He was able to understand a young man, ambitious,
wanting to get ahead. That taught me a lesson—
that in developing personality one must develop
broad sympathies toward everyone no matter from
what station in life he comes.

Another thing I noticed in great personalities
with whom I have come into contact is that they
always develop a characteristic of leadership. Not
only in big things but in little things. For instance,
I have noticed if I meet a really big man and
walk only a few blocks with him he gives me something stimulating to think about. It may be one of
his own problems or one of my problems or the
question of how to help put over the Community
Fund this year, or next month's business program,

or church program, or any kind of program—but
he has led my mind and me into a new realm. It's
a pretty good rule to remember that every time
we come into contact with another person, even
though just walking a block, our job is to lead him
to a higher plane than that one on which we found
him.

The other day a young friend of mine called and
congratulated me on my wedding anniversary.
When he went out of his way to do this little courtesy, it reminded me of another quality which great
personalities have—that of thoughtfulness. Incidentally, this young man is rapidly developing a
fine personality. I reflected that this quality of
thoughtfulness for others was one of the reasons
why. We cannot go on a glorious crusade and forget
the fellow crusader who is marching at our elbows.
We cannot develop personality if we entirely ignore
the man at the desk across from us. In thinking
of the big things of life don't overlook the little
things because this quality of thoughtfulness is
mainly concerned with little things. I have always
found a notebook has been my best help to develop
this trait of thoughtfulness. Record birthdays, anni-
versaries, children's names, interesting events.
When you make a new contact it doesn't take long
to write a note showing that you appreciated it. It
isn't any gift you send, it's the thought that
goes with it that endears you to others. Thoughtfulness is a giving of yourself. It's easy to pick up
a telephone and wish your associate in business
Godspeed on the journey he is undertaking. That

doesn't take much of your time, but how it increases the zest with which he undertakes that journey. You only have to leave for the office five minutes earlier to drop by the hospital to see that acquaintance who is ill. Ten minutes tonight, before you eat your dinner, spent in writing a longhand note to your very gracious host of the other night will cement a friendship that will mean much to you and to the host. A millionaire in money is nothing compared to being a millionaire in friends, and everyone can be this, provided you keep these friends when you make them. And thoughtfulness in little things is the best way I know to keep them.

There are many more qualities which one can use to develop personality. These are just some of the outstanding ones. You yourself must have learned the things that build up this social side of your life. There is one other, however, before we close this chapter, which I believe will prove very valuable in your life. That is to treat everybody alike, no matter from what station in life he comes. Be your own self with all people whether they be prince or pauper. This may sound like a bromide, but look around you at the people you know. Unfortunately, there are many people in the world so constituted that they are always licking the boots of those over them and lording it over those under them. That's a sure way to destroy personality. On the other hand, really great men and women are those who are natural, frank and honest with everyone with whom they come into contact.

For a long time I have been going to the Gulf
Coast each winter to shoot ducks. In the blinds you
spend a lot of time thinking and waiting. Often I find
myself wondering what it is in the fall that starts
these wild ducks and other migratory birds on their
long journey from the Hudson Bay in the Northland
clear down to the Gulf Coast and even farther.
And then in the spring, what starts them back
North again. Is it some inner urge that whispers
timidly at first as the leaves begin to turn? And then
does it grow and grow with the wintry blasts into an
overwhelming obsession until it governs every
action of the bird and finally sends it on its long
migration across the continent? Or is it only in
the restless breast of the leader that the urge to go
becomes an all-consuming one? Is he the one that
persuades the others that *now* is the time to get up
and go? At any rate, something happens to all
Duckland. Something so urgent and so irresistible
that not a single duck can disregard it. Old ducks,
young ducks, weak ducks, strong ducks—they all
go and fly as far as they have strength toward their
destination because of some daring urge within
them.

That's the kind of urge you must possess. Something so overwhelming that you can't resist it. A
"Magnificent Obsession" that wakes you in the
morning with a desire to serve that cannot be put
aside. Something that sends you into any group,
not with the thought, "what can I get out of them,"
but rather with "what can I give."

It is this social side of life where our principle
that valuable possessions when shared multiply
becomes doubly effective. Here truly the more you
give the more you are capable of giving. I dare
you to develop the fine art of finding, making, and
keeping friends by genuine giving of your time and
personality to others. Look for the best in people.
Learn to like people. Find out what they are
interested in. Select five new people this month.
Show yourself friendly to each one by giving them
some particular little courtesy. Then watch what
happens. At the end of the month, you have five
new friends—and inside a deeper capacity for
friendship and a richer personality.

You can be bigger socially than you have ever
been in your life. That's sure. In the social realm
results are immediately evident because every day
you are reacting on others. You can't grow socially
unless you help others grow also. My social Dares
are so simple—right down to earth.

I dare you, Winning Smile, to replace Old Man
Grouch.

I dare you, Mr. Snapping Turtle, to depart to
another climate.

I dare you, Flabby Fingers, to develop into a
Warm Handclasp.

I dare you, my own Personality, to become a
Welcome Guest everywhere.

I dare you, my Social Self, to generate that
Magnetic Spark which leads to a charmed life.

To accomplish these Dares and possess that intangible something which attracts people, I would suggest definite consideration of the following questions, which should be written down on a sheet of paper and stuck in your mirror. When you have answers that show definite progress, add those to the sheet.

1. Am I a greater or lesser factor in my community than I was a year or two years ago?

1. What is my program?

2. Was there ever a time in my life when I was contributing more to the welfare of others than I am now?

2. What are my aggressive plans?

3. Is the level of my friendship up from a year ago —or down?

3. How to make more and better friends plans.

4. Are jealousy, grouchiness, bad temper, or any other social handicaps increasing or decreasing in my life?

4. My plans for stamping them out.

5. Is it possible to picture any other environment under which I would increase my accomplishments?

5. What is this improved environment?

6. What's My Big Social Dare?

6. When shall it be Daringly Done?

7. Dare I dare to become like some great outstanding personality?

7. Progress.

I DARE YOU TO BUILD CHARACTER

We were climbing up the great trail toward the mountain peak. Jimmy, our five-year-old grandson, was struggling to keep up.

"Tired, Jimmy?" I asked.

"My feet are tired but myself isn't," he answered.

"Myself" was Jimmy's spirit. Up the Great Trail was an adventure for five-year-old Jimmy. Up the Great Trail will be an adventure for twenty-year-old Jimmy—yes, for thirty-year-old Jimmy and fifty-year-old Jimmy. As long as the spirit is there, Jimmy will continue to climb. Tired? Yes, of course, he will become tired. Yes, of course, body will be tired, but Jimmy's spirit never tires of urging him to higher and higher plateaus.

There is an old Hindu legend, says Claude Bragdon, that at one time all men on earth were gods, but that men so sinned and abused the Divine that Brahma, the god of all gods, decided that the godhead should be taken away from man and hid some place where they would never again find it to abuse it. "We will bury it deep in the earth," said the other gods. "No," said Brahma, "because man will dig down in the earth and find it." "Then we will sink it in the deepest ocean," they said. "No," said Brahma, "because man will learn to dive and find it there, too." "We will hide it on the highest mountain," they said. "No," said Brahma, "because man will some day climb every mountain on the earth and again capture the godhead." "Then we do not know where to hide it where he cannot find it," said the lesser gods. "I will tell you," said Brahma. "hide it down in man himself. He will never think to look there."

And that is what they did. Hidden down in every man is some of the divine. Ever since then he has gone over the earth digging, diving and climbing, looking for that godlike quality which all the time is hidden down within himself.

It is this spark that I am daring you to turn into a blaze.—"It is this radiance we must recapture." It is something genuine, something for everyday use. It is the spirit that naturally makes you do the right thing at the right time.

It's the thing that makes a gentleman and a gentlewoman. It is that unseen something that will not let you take advantage of a weaker person, whether it be on the football field or in a business transaction. It is that something inside of every worth while person that makes him decide right when temptation confronts him, be fair, be honest, and be dependable. And this spirit I am talking about is not one that skulks back in the shadows. It is one that belongs up with the captains and kings. It is a spirit proud of its heritage, one that flies its banner high.

Too much has been left to the preachers in the past. The day has gone when the radiant side of life can be located like a Sunday suit and only put on one day a week. I am still speaking to you as a practical business man, daring you to live a complete life. What General would attack on three fronts and retreat on the fourth? Would you be fair to yourself to quit with three-fourths victory when complete victory is in sight? During the summer I sat high up on the sand dunes of our American Youth Foundation Camp in Michigan and watched the ever-changing glory of Lake Michigan by day and night. Sunrises and sunsets. Moon and stars. Water and sky that were never the same. But the thing that gripped me most was the horizon line. Some days it would be miles and miles away. On other days a mist would turn into a fog, and my horizon was just a stone's throw away. Who wants to live in a fog and be limited in his outreach? I know of no other side of life that will so widen your whole horizon as the development of this last and most important frontier.

It is to you, strong of body, brilliant of mind, magnetic in personality, that I am talking now. What price all of these without the inspiration of a Cause? Since the beginning of things, man has had the capacity for some kind of spiritual life. Unless this side is developed, it dies, and all the other three sides of life suffer. No man can allow part of himself to die without penalizing the parts of him which continue to live. If attack is the keynote of growth in our physical, mental, and social lives, why not in the spiritual life, too?

I remember a dear old lady whose life was a constant benediction, sitting in a group where everyone but herself seemed picking to pieces the church, religion, and finally even Christ Himself. Like an avenging angel she suddenly stood over them, silencing their chatter with words that pierced like swords. "How dare you criticize my Lord!" she demanded. And they all wondered how they had dared. You couldn't criticize General Washington with Anthony Wayne in the room. Who would dare say anything about Pasteur with any of his co-workers standing by? Why should any Spiritual Crusader sit passive when the Crusader of Galilee will take us on an adventure far beyond our fondest dreams?

Strength and courage are essential in the development of the physical, mental, and social sides of life. Aren't you willing to admit that you need these qualities on your spiritual front as well? Look at the Honor Roll of Christ's Crusaders. Are there any weaklings there? Saul of Tarsus persecuted the Christians until a light from heaven changed his whole life and he became Paul, the preacher, who stormed the very gates of Rome under the shadow of Death itself, to carry his Master's message to the needy. Was there any lack of adventure in his life? Peter, fiery and impetuous, was unwilling for Christ to wash his feet. In his human weakness, he denied his Lord thrice. That same Peter, who caught the passion of service, was crucified head downwards. Whoever fought against greater odds to more far-reaching victories than those Spiritual Crusaders of old!

"What is a spiritual adventure?" you ask.

Here is a striking example. In St. Paul's Cathedral, London, on a tablet to the memory of General Charles Gordon—"Chinese Gordon"—I read these immortal words:

> "Who at all times and everywhere gave
> His Strength to the Weak
> His Substance to the Poor
> His Sympathy to the Suffering
> His Heart to God."

Sir Wilfred Grenfell found, too, that all spiritual adventure had for its foundation first the giving of one's loyalty to a living leader and then expressing it in knightly service. "Real religion involves real courage," he writes. "The inefficiency which I had associated with it had not been its fault, but ours. We had not dreamt of taking Christ in earnest— religion makes one do things—a power beyond my own to win out."

I am not asking you to become preachers like Paul or Peter, or a soldier like Gordon, or a medical missionary like Grenfell, but I am asking you to consider their revolutionary idea of making an adventure out of their religion. These men, with thoughts so like our very own, first fell into the false notion that religion was something for young children or old people, or for the weak or sickly,

or the fanatics. But how different when they
found that it was a power that worked in every
phase of their own lives, building the physical,
developing the mental, inspiring the social.

Maybe Sir Wilfred Grenfell's method of attack
on the spiritual front will help us. He says in his
book, "What Christ Means to Me": "If the hardest
thing in the world to resist is temptation, we should
present a vision of Christ that tempts men the right
way. Real religion dreams and sees visions that
intoxicate, every bit as much as the license per-
mitted by the will not to believe. Only it intoxi-
cates with deeds of kindness, justice, chivalry, love.
It answers the insatiate demands of youth and high
spirit for freedom from boredom and the pettiness
of daily routine every whit as naturally and unde-
niably as dram-drinking, petting parties, gaming
tables, or the self-pollution of lust and license which
surely, if slowly, evoke the loathsome Hyde out of
the knightly Jekyll which is in us. . . .

"Paul's life was as full of thrills as Herod
Agrippa's, Livingstone's and Lincoln's, as Jay
Gould's or King Charles II's. Christ means to me
the best kind of a Friend, as well as Leader. If
Christ is right and life is a field of honor, and Sir
Galahad and Nathan Hale and Edith Cavell got the
real fun out of it, then to every red-blooded man
life becomes heaven in proportion as he seizes its
opportunities for service."

This is from a man who saw life as a whole. In
Labrador he became the great healer and the great
lover of men. He made new men as well as new

legs.   He made the morally lame, as well as the physically lame, walk straight once more.

Doing right can be made actually more thrilling than doing wrong.   Our Labrador hero has proven this by his daring deeds.   The lure of the Labrador Wild was his spiritual adventure.   You who risk the remorse of tomorrow for tonight's thrill, why not try the Grenfell kind of thrill that brings joy instead of remorse?

Lift your thoughts above the commonplace. Think on noble things.   Soon you are on a higher level.   If you consider religion something to be put up with, it becomes a drudgery.   Exercise and study are a drudgery to one in the wrong mental attitude. But if you consider the building of character, or ethics, or morals, or religion—whatever you choose to call it—as an opportunity to grow, then the unseen things of life take on a new significance. My inspiring friend, Dr. Charles R. Brown, Dean Emeritus of Yale Theological Seminary, told my co-workers at our mill that he judges a man by his wants.   If you don't want to be a spiritual adventurer, you never will.   But if you sear into your brain and heart and soul a hunger for the best of life, a craving to grow, a cause for your crusade, then you have already advanced on the fourth front.

Dare to live in the Presence of the Best.   Try for one week to live a distinguished life, surrounding yourself with the very best the world has to offer. Read an excellent poem.   Begin the biography of a distinguished man.   Study a painting by an Old

Master. Hear a best Victrola record. Listen to a
classical radio program or a symphony. See an
uplifting play or movie. Hear a stirring speaker.
Meet an inspiring personality. See a sunrise and a
sunset. Strive to crowd out of your life unworthy
thoughts, unworthy acts, unworthy contacts. Just
see what will happen if, for a solid week, you fill
your life only with the best!—the very best in litera-
ture, the very best in art, the very best in nature. If
only we would surround ourselves with the world's
excellence, we would live like Kings!

Physical strength demands exercise. **Mental
alertness demands study. Winsome personality
thrives on service. Religious growth requires
action,** the actual doing of right things instead of the
wrong. We advance only by doing.

Say your prayers tonight, but unless tomorrow
you can act on them, they are not worth much. **Dr.
E. Stanley Jones** in his book, "The Christ of Every
Road," tells the following story:

"I once came down from Almore over one of the
worst winding roads of the world. The driver of
the bus had never driven in the Himalayas before,
and it happened that on his first trip the previous
day he had almost gone over one of those terrifying
precipitous cliffs. He was nervous; so before starting back he came in front of the engine and stood
with folded hands, saying his prayers to the
machine. That done, we started off, but had not
gone far when the engine began to overheat. There
was no water in the radiator! This was remedied.
But when we were still many miles from our

destination, the machine stopped while going up a hill. There was no petrol in the tank! There we stayed until rescued. The driver said his prayers to the machine, but put no water in the radiator and no petrol in the tank."

Why not start an offensive today? Couldn't you begin by putting your prayers into action? What definite right things will you do to replace some of the wrong things you have been doing? What particular hill will you take? Will you set a zero hour to go over some top that has stood as an obstacle in your life? List some of these things, and opposite them launch an offensive program. Imagine yourself a Paul or a Peter, or a Gordon, or a Grenfell, or that quiet friend of yours who is like the still waters that run deep, but whose life overflows with good deeds which bring rewards beyond measure. Better still, make a program that will be satisfied with nothing less than *your own self at your very best all the time.*

A thrilling spiritual adventure awaits you but it will take courage. The men who dared were the first pioneers to cross the wilderness. They were the front line men in the great war. Courage challenged their inner resources. You cannot climb your spiritual heights without that same courage to loosen the powers that fare within you.

Don't be discouraged if you fail in your first efforts. Coach Meehan of New York University says, "We learn practically nothing from a victory.

All our information comes from a defeat. A winner
forgets most of his mistakes."

At the Northfield Student Conference, the West
Point delegation was holding a little group meeting
in a dimly lighted tent. "What is Christianity?"
was one of the perplexing questions that was asked.
There was a moment's silence; then from a dark
corner came an inspired answer: "Christianity?
Why, Christianity is Oscar Westover." How one
would like to have known him—a West Point cadet
whose life had so commended his religion to his
mates that in his absence he should be offered by
one of them and accepted by the rest as a working
definition of the living embodiment of the Christian
religion.

Paul said to his young friend, Timothy, "Where-
fore I put thee in remembrance that thou *stir up
the gift of God* which is within thee."

It is not for me to tell you what your spiritual
Dare should be. You know your own life. There
is just one big thing I Dare you to do—Beat Your
Best. Spiritual investments are repaid a thousand-
fold. Don't worry about your few little loaves.
Invest what you have. The returns will be far
more than you realize. Catch some great challenge
of service. Men do great deeds under a "Magnificent Obsession."

If you will write out the following questions and answer them carefully, it will help clarify your spiritual dares.

1. I have read Fosdick's "Twelve Tests of Character" and will grade myself.

2. Am I above or below the average on moral courage?

3. How dependable am I?—how honest?

4. Was God ever more real to me than He is today?

5. My spiritual self is my greatest possession. Plan for its growth. What am I going to do to develop it this year?

   What crusade am I going to send it on next year?

6. What is my great Spiritual Dare?

7. Have I a great Cause in Life? A Magnificent Obsession?

Record your progress by writing the following questions on a sheet of paper. Then Dare to grade yourself. You will not want to stop until you have lifted yourself to your highest levels of satisfaction.

1. Twelve Tests Tested.

   Grade after three months.

2. What one thing have I done to improve my moral courage?

3. How have I dared to improve my dependability?

   My honesty?

4. What is my definite program for growth?

5. In what way have I shown spiritual growth during the past three months?

6. What have I done toward accomplishing my spiritual Dare?

7. Is my Cause any nearer accomplishment than it was three months ago?

I DARE YOU TO SHARE

Many of you have read Lloyd C. Douglas' "Magnificent Obsession." The plot is most unique and reveals in a most interesting way how a young man, with all the graces that one could desire, learned the secret of real social growth. He was rich and lived a spoiled, useless life, when an accident brought him up with a jolt. He recovered consciousness in a hospital to find he had been almost drowned. His life had been saved, however, by means of a pulmotor rushed over from the summer cottage of a world-famous brain surgeon. The unfortunate tragedy was that the surgeon was drowned while the pulmotor which could have saved his life was being used to save the ne'er-do-well. The story tells how the young man, realizing he had been indirectly responsible for the loss to the world of a great man, resolved to fill this great man's place by becoming an equally capable brain surgeon, himself. That resolution became his Obsession, and eventually he accomplished his aim. But in so doing he discovered his "Magnificent Obsession." He found he must become more than a brain surgeon to fill the eminent man's shoes. The famous doctor had been an even greater personality in an entirely different sphere of life. Literally thousands

of people had been helped in various ways by him.
To some he had given money, to others his time, to
others his skill. But always on one condition, that
they should never during his lifetime reveal the
fact of his help. His Theory had been that in giving
of his possessions to others, unknown to the world,
he was contributing to his own personality—that
unheralded good deeds enlarged and enriched life.
The story goes on to tell how the young man, filled
with this "Magnificent Obsession," practiced the
same theory and marched on to the same reward.

I would hate to think something tragic would
be necessary to put a Magnificent Obsession into
your life. The young man in the story found his
urge when he discovered his aimless life had been
saved at the expense of a worthy one. Then he
dared to give back to the world what he had caused
the world to lose. You are enjoying something
today because of others' sacrifices. Doesn't that
dare you to make good?

If one is to share properly he cannot shirk the
responsibility of service. Community Funds, Red
Cross drives have to be done by someone. Years
ago when I was down in the Bahama Islands I found
a red bean which the natives believed was the omen
of good luck. I have carried those beans with me
for many, many years and with them I founded
what I like to call "The Good Turn Bean Society
of the World." When one does me a really good
turn I give him one of these red beans and make
him a member of the Society. You would be sur-
prised how many quarts of these beans I have sent

for to replenish my supply. It just seems the whole world is made up of people who do good turns. Unless we want to be parasites we must do more good turns than others do to us. Because we are leaders and crusaders we are daring to attempt more than the other fellow. What time and thought and energy are we giving to community needs, to welfare work, to church activities? All of these services must be done by someone not for pay. Pay comes in rich full measure by sharing.

"We Florentines," says one of George Eliot's characters, "live scrupulously that we may spend splendidly."

Another illustration I believe expresses this idea of sharing with others is the one used by Dr. Fosdick in "The Meaning of Service."

"The Sea of Galilee and the Dead Sea are made of the same water. It flows down, clear and cool, from the Hermon and the roots of the cedars of Lebanon. The Sea of Galilee makes beauty of it, for the Sea of Galilee has an outlet. *It gets to give.* It gathers in its riches that it may pour them out again to fertilize the Jordan plain. But the Dead Sea, with the same water, makes horror. For the Dead Sea has no outlet. It gets to keep. That is the radical difference between selfish and unselfish men. We all do want life's enriching blessings; we ought to; they are divine benedictions. But some men get to give, and they are like Galilee; while some men get to keep and they are like the brackish water that covers Sodom and Gomorrah."

Let me tell you two true stories of sharing. One
about the Richest Little Rich Girl I ever knew
and the other about the Richest Little Poor Girl
that I ever knew.

Mary Brendon's father was a rich steel manufac-
turer in the East. Of course, Mary Brendon isn't
her real name. If I told you exactly who she was,
she would scalp me. She had everything in the
world she wanted—money, clothes, luxuries, everything. The World War came. She was determined
to go to France. Her father was equally determined
that she shouldn't. She won. Fathers have a great
way of backing down, but not too graciously. She
was accepted by the Y. M. C. A. With her violin—
for she was an accomplished musician—she was
off for overseas. I had charge of the Y work in the
old Third Division, a unit of the regular army under
Major General Joseph F. Dickman. We were in
training at Chateau Villain. We had the best group
of Y. M. C. A. workers in France. I acknowledge
that. But we didn't have nearly enough. At the
Y headquarters in Paris I was considered hard-
boiled. Any weak or just ordinary, mediocre
workers they would send down, I'd fire right
back. You see, I was too old to enlist, had been a
business man all my life, with experience in picking
men, and I got into the Y because I wanted to do
my share. Anyway, a bit of fighting and adventure
were always to my liking. But one day Mary
Brendon arrived with her violin under her arm.
She brought a note from my friend, Helen King,
who assigned all the girls, saying that she would

stick. Mary looked as if a strong puff of wind would blow her away, but there she stood, clinging to her violin. There were no easy jobs. She was placed with the old Seventh Infantry. I get a shudder up my back now as I think of the work those girls did. They scrubbed their canteens, made literally barrels of hot chocolate, washed endless dishes. I'll bet Mary never washed a dish in all her life before. At night the men were entertained—and scant entertainment it was, too. Mary was everywhere, always with her violin, striking up a tune. How her boys could sing, and how they adored her! And well they might for the way she fought for supplies for her men. She would get so insistent at times that I wanted to send her back to Paris, but she had handled her father at home, and in her quiet way had learned to get what she wanted.

Our great day came. We were ordered to the front. Mary wouldn't be left behind. She followed her men right up to the Marne. The day before we were ordered into the lines for our first baptism of fire, our chaplains, Protestants and Catholics, planned communion for our men. There weren't chaplains enough to be everywhere. I pressed all our Y preachers into service. Poor little Mary was out of luck. She loved her men. She knew many of them would never come back, but we couldn't find a chaplain or minister for her anywhere; so she must go without communion. But not so, Mary. "Please help me, Mr. Danforth," she pleaded. "I'll get the bread and wine and I'll play a hymn on my violin, and we will serve our men ourselves." And she did, bless her heart! Never in my life has a communion made such an impression on me.

July fifteenth and sixteenth, 1918, were awful days for the old Third Division. The Germans were driven back over the Marne, but our losses were terrific. Y trucks were turned into ambulances. Y men did heroic work. Never did our Y girls falter. Pressed into service at the dressing stations, Mary Brendon and the other girls cared for the wounded without batting an eye. Major General Dickman recognized such service on behalf of the Third Division Y with a beautiful citation. I could tell you a lot more about this Rich Little Rich Girl, but you know enough to catch the spiritual uplift of such a life.

Rich, talented, hard working, courageous—yes, all of these. But she gave something more. It was Mary's spirit that lived in the hearts of all with whom she worked. She had offered her life in the service of her country and her God. She was working for a *Cause*, an all-consuming passion for service absorbed her. And in her sharing what she had with others a richer life came back to her.

It is this same kind of Cause, a similar urge and a similar sharing, that I dare you to put into your heart and soul.

Now let me tell you about my Rich Little Poor Girl. I'll name her Ruth Adams. Of course, that isn't her name. If she ever reads this, even without her name, she will protest to the heavens that there isn't a word of truth in my story. But by so doing

she would be running true to form. To be strictly
truthful, Ruth was neither rich nor poor. Her father
was a professional man, and she was a strong and
happy daughter, full of ideas which could not all be
worked out in New England. The Great War was
over. The Near East Relief was caring for orphans
and refugees in that hotbed of racial strife—Turkey,
Armenia and Greece. The need was great. Self-
sacrificing workers were few. Ruth Adams had
been in the Near East before. She knew there was
dirt and rags and typhus at the other end. Long
hours, sickness, death—some never came back! No
glamour of war. Nothing heroic about it—just a
dirty, complicated job of trying to save children
while politics and war broke down homes and killed
off families who had every right to live. An inner
urge possessed Ruth Adams. My, how it gets you.
She would go!

I visited the Barracks in Constantinople. The
sight of the refugees pouring in beggars description.
Those who survived, weary and weak after their
long trek, fell across the threshold. They were
huddled into over - crowded, ill - ventilated rooms.
The next morning those who died during the night
were laid in piles like cordwood and carted away.
The sight was worse than war, and I know war.
Helpless women and children, hope gone, strength
gone, dying like rats — such scenes wrung our
hearts. Here Ruth Adams worked. A barracks
in her charge was ordered evacuated. Turkish soldiers cleared the building and reported that no one
was left. Ruth didn't believe them. She would

see for herself. On the top floor she found two women and a little child, who looked like a four or five-year-old, but who turned out to be eight years old. She demanded that they be removed. "No use; they will die before morning and we'll cart them away. Save handling twice." That was the soldiers' reply. Roused to special effort because of the injustice and neglect of these refugees, Ruth Adams gave all the strength she possessed, and with only a driver's help, carried the women from the top floor to the car. Then she returned and in her own arms brought that little unconscious bundle of a girl down herself. She rushed them to the American Hospital in Stamboul. Hoping against hope, she laid the little child on a hospital bed and begged the nurses, as a final gesture, to pretend that the child had a chance to survive. She persuaded them to bathe and feed her as tenderly as a convalescent who needs personal care for recovery, even though they knew all too well that they had little more than a corpse. Ruth left the hospital, rushing back to her work, knowing that her friends, the nurses, would do their utmost. They did and the child is alive today, miraculously saved.

Within a week Ruth Adams was brought into the same hospital. The dreaded typhus had caught her. She fought through weeks of unconsciousness, with expert care of doctors and nurses. Her indomitable spirit, together with their skill and a merciful Providence, pulled her through. I met her at the Mission when she was convalescing. Her pale cheeks told of her struggle, but she had the

flash of fire in her eyes. She asked to talk to me.
Here is what she said:

"Mr. Danforth, you have some influence, haven't
you? Please, Mr. Danforth, urge the doctors to let
me go back to my work. I'm strong enough. Those
faces haunt me. They need my help. I can do a
lot if I can only go back..."

Such pleading I never expect to hear again. I
thought of my own daughter with her little children
back home. I knew she would plead in the same
way. The spirit can't be quenched, but what can
a weak body do until strength and health are
restored?

"No, Ruth," I said, "you can't go back to your
work now. Your life has been miraculously spared
for great days ahead. Obey the doctor's orders.
Be a good soldier." She leaned back in her weak
condition, crestfallen.

There's much more to this story, but I've told
enough. This girl used the energy she had in her,
for she loved people, whether well, sick, rich, poor,
in trouble, or out of it. She lived the abundant
life of service. "She worked as if everything
depended on her. She had faith as if everything
depended on God."

How vividly such sharing adventures stand out
in our memories. Riches or poverty are forgotten.
Even Health and Mentality and Social Graces step
aside before such devotion to an unselfish cause.
I dare you to take your place among such of life's
immortals as my Rich Little Rich Girl and my Rich
Little Poor Girl. Make a masterpiece of your life.

And when you have dared to develop this ability
to share with others you have discovered the meaning of an abundant life. Following the principle
that *our most valuable possessions are those which
can be shared without lessening, those which,
when shared, multiply; our least valuable possessions are those which, when divided, are diminished,*
then truly our physical, mental, social and spiritual
selves multiply many times over when they are
shared.

The more you practice this principle of daring
and sharing, the more you find it in every contact
of life. I heard my beloved pastor, Doctor Jay T.
Stocking, who has now gone to his rich reward,
preach a remarkable sermon on "The Investment
of Life." He told the story of the loaves and fishes,
but with a new interpretation. He stressed not the
miracle of feeding the four thousand with a few
loaves, but the attitude that takes account of
resources possessed rather than of difficulties presented. "Measure your powers, not your problems."
What a dare in these adventurous days! When the
disciples counted the crowd and petulantly com-
plained that a few loaves were not enough to feed
the multitudes, Jesus said, "How many loaves have
ye? Don't look at the hillside—look at the basket.
Don't count the crowd—count the loaves." He did
not minimize the task. He suggested that if they
could not feed four thousand people, they could at
least satisfy the hunger of a few. They made a
beginning and in using what they had under His
direction, they acquired more than they had.

"We arrive here at a universal law of life and of God," said Dr. Stocking, "that resources and powers are given to those who use what resources and powers they have. Through the use of our muscles, our muscles grow and harden. Through the use of our mind, mental capacity increases; through the use of our spiritual powers these powers heighten. We do not wear out the mind with thinking, or the soul with loving and showing mercy. It is within the experience of all of us that through using what we have we become possessed of larger abilities and resources—'Don't count the multitude. Count the loaves.'"

Mahatma Gandhi never asks men for more than they can give, but he asks for all they can give.

I heard my friend, President Emeritus Wm. J. Hutchins of Berea College, give these thoughts to a graduating class.

"A few men build cities—the rest live in them.

"A few men project subways—the rest ride in them.

"A few men erect skyscrapers and factories—and the rest toil in them."

This book is written to you few who are going to accomplish things. You few who will dare to pioneer. You few who will dream of foundations and great super-structures to satisfy the needs of mankind. The rest will follow your leadership. You are the shepherds—the rest are the sheep. The shepherd loves his sheep. He faces danger. He knows hardship. There are stray lambs. He brings them back. Close your eyes and say to yourself, "I am one of the few. I have a leader's opportunity. I have a shepherd's responsibility. The rest are dependent upon me."

I'LL DARE TO SHARE WITH OTHERS

1. What talents have I which I could share with others?

2. In what way am I sharing *my* loaves with others?

3. How will I dare to use the life I have and share it with others?

4. Outline on a sheet of paper for myself a definite sharing program which I will start tomorrow.

LAUNCH OUT INTO THE DEEP

The four-square life that I've dared you to live isn't easy—*it is hard*. The masses—the 95%—will be content to go along their own way. Their plateau is comfortable. Why be disturbed or excited? But that other 4% and the Kingly 1% will never be

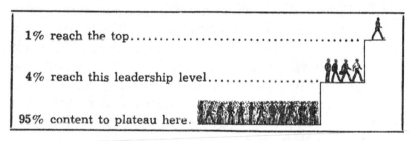

1% reach the top.......................................

4% reach this leadership level...................

95% content to plateau here.

held down until every unused capacity has been marshalled for service. What is it that lights the fuse of the 4% to the higher Leadership level and then that other 1% to the Kingly group? Why do the 95% never get their second wind? If the habits of the 95% keep them on their plateau, don't you think by grim determination, you, with your marvelous unused capacities, can form just as strong a habit to live on the 4% Leadership level or rise to the Kingly 1%? But it takes real stuff to do it.

When I sailed through the Caribbean Sea, I became steeped in the stories of old Panama. Why

seek the Pacific beyond when there were treasures
enough to spare on this side. But there was
"something more" on the far shore...a new ocean
to sail and the gold of the Incas! In between was
that impenetrable Isthmus. There came Totten, the
engineer, who spent five long years of untold difficulties and discouragement in building a railroad
across that Isthmus. Through dense jungles infested
by pestilential dangers, mosquitoes, flies, snakes,
miasma everywhere in slimy ooze. "Every tie in
the Panama Railroad represents the life of some
man who paid the price of its construction with his
life." Totten was stricken with yellow fever. For
days he lingered between life and death. His
Spanish doctor said there was no hope. Totten
roused himself, and with that same indomitable
courage that had marked his every step, said, "You
are mistaken, sir; not yet. Yellow fever can't kill
a Totten. I'm going to get well!" And he did. 4%
and 1% stuff in him!

Then came the digging of the canal. DeLesseps,
the famous Frenchman, had failed. The world said,
"It can't be done." America purchased the Isthmus.
President Theodore Roosevelt appointed George W.
Goethals to build the canal. He had the reputation
of never quitting. The world flippantly said, "Let
George do it." Colonel Goethals "put to the full test
the fearless courage that was the measure of the
man." The canal was completed. "George did it."
No 95% plateau levels for this George.

But George didn't do it without the help of
another fearless man. William C. Gorgas, an Amer-

ican Army doctor, was selected to fight malaria and yellow fever. He scanned the record of twenty thousand who had died from these pestilential diseases. One report showed that five hundred young engineers came from France to Panama and "not one lived to draw his first month's pay." Then began Dr. Gorgas' most amazing campaign. He was ridiculed, called a mosquito chaser; but Gorgas "concentrated his sleepless energies upon one single aim—the destruction of the infecting mosquitoes, and he won what was unquestionably the greatest triumph in preventive medicine. A campaign waged for less than six months wiped out a scourge that had afflicted this region for at least four hundred years." Had he allowed ridicule and opposition to overcome his courage, the Panama Canal might not have been built.

Courage for your tasks. That's what's needed. Courage of the lasting kind, too. Many start. Few finish. Many "mount up with wings like eagles" but only the select few continue to "walk without fainting."

You adventurous spirits will meet obstacles, but dare to map out a program of life with a sense of direction, but with no sense of obstacles.

Alexander the Great heard of India's fabulous wealth and splendor. There he would go. He had no maps but he had an objective and a sense of direction. Rivers and mountains and warlike nations had no terrors for him. Through the Khyber Pass he went with no sense of obstacles. His eyes were on his destination.

Caesar saw Britain—not the gruelling marches, treacherous tribes, and danger on every hand between him and his goal. He had an objective and a sense of direction. Napoleon saw Italy but not the Alps. Washington saw the Hessians at Trenton. A smaller man would have seen the ice-filled Delaware.

The 95% see the obstacles. The 4% and the 1% see the objective. Small men painstakingly survey the first obstacle which dwarfs their natures and foreshortens their vision. Great men with a sense of direction have that confidence and determination which trample obstacles under foot.

History records the successes of men with objectives and a sense of direction. Oblivion is the position of small men overwhelmed by obstacles.

Living the Four-Square life through your Dares gives you a sense of direction and sweeps obstacles out of your path. Your adventurous life has just begun. It takes more than saying you are going to do it to achieve. Theodore Roosevelt said, "There must be more shooting and less shouting; fewer words and more real work. Words will not plow a field; words will not build a home; words will not develop a great humanity, nor build a great nation." There is discipline ahead. Walking with the army and wearing a uniform doesn't make a man a soldier.

Dare to make a start. All the plans in the world will not help you so much as one small deed. This book will not have served its purpose unless it *starts you* living the complete life. It is human to put things off. It is divine to start things off. Your daring program begins not next month, not next week, not even tomorrow. I dare you to begin to live the Four-Square life today.

There's Hero Stuff in you. I dare you to get it out. Use your imagination as you read this football dope.

"...and the coach kicks every man out on the field and tells him to go to it. He keeps right on working them back and forth until their tongues hang out and they think they can't make another down. Then he works them some more, and some more, and finally ends up in a sprint around the track.

"The result is that every man brings out everything that is in him. The fast and fearless step into their strides and replace the halfbacks that aren't any good. Finally there is a great team and a great game and a great score. And the man who made those two touchdowns on that muddy day in November becomes a Hero and stays one all the rest of his life and every man on the team is proud."

"Pass the ball to me," do I hear you say? Pass it to you with those weights on your shoulders and shackles on your feet which prevent you from moving? No sir! The man with the ball must be in fighting trim. Go back to those inflexible rules of the four-square life in the preceding chapters. Master them. Get on the Varsity Team of life. Face your tasks. Launch out. Take the risk. Dare to do.

I would encourage many little Dares. You will need them to bolster up that one great, big, all-

absorbing Dare of your life. Let me look you
squarely in the eyes, hear your Dare, and learn of
the purpose behind it, and I'll gamble I can take
your measure. If I see the light of battle in your
eyes and catch something of a dominant inner urge,
then I know you are on your way.

Many are good starters but poor finishers. The
streets are full of people who started out but fell
by the wayside. "This man began to build, but was
not able to finish." Launching your ship is a gala
occasion, but the storms and waves are the tests.
"I'm afraid you won't be able to make it," whispers
a little Imp who constantly tries to poison your
mind. Knock such fears galley-west. Those who
dare take risks, but so do those who do not dare—
not the risks of shipwreck and failure, but the risks
of rust and decay. Do you remember the story of
the Covered Wagon crossing the plains toward the
Golden West?—

> "The Coward never started;
> The Weak died on the way;
> Only the Strong came through!"

There will be times when you will want to quit,
when you will consign me and my dares to a
warmer climate. But you can't quit. You have
unused capacities that cry out within you. You are
made of 4% Leadership stuff — yes, maybe you
belong to the Kingly 1%. John Paul Jones, when
ordered to surrender, said, "We've just begun to
fight!" Did Admiral Farragut weaken with hidden
mines in his path? "Damn the topedoes. Full

steam ahead!" was his command. Determination to win decides the issue. During the war in France, one of our officers, after being asked the question, "Can we hold them?" answered, "Can we hold them? We will go through them and smash them."

May I say again that the real cause of strength under baffling conditions comes right back to your four-square life. That's the secret I must tell. Those four hard chapters contain the very heart of life. I have seen the test come in business and in war. In my Division in France we had some Tennessee mountain boys. When Hell was turned loose they were bewildered. They knew two things, however; they knew their rifles and they knew how to shoot straight. When fundamentals begin to grip you, when you have made the four-square life your life, all Hell may break, but you will dare to reach your goal.

Let me finish this chapter by again impressing on you from a business point of view what I've tried to say in the preceding pages.

Capitalize four square living just as bankers or manufacturers capitalize their assets. Use your physical strength. Put it behind your dare. Keep enough in reserve for emergencies. You can go far using your teeming physical energy. Corral your brain power. When you have learned to face facts and think straight, you can mix brains with that fine body of yours and have two arrows to shoot. Making friends and holding them by a winsome personality along with an alert mind and strong body, you have three powers at your command.

You who dare, don't waste. The four-fold life is
yours because underneath a body which is under
control and a mind keen as a brier and a personality
that sparkles at every contact, there is a religion
with truth, honesty and purity as its base.

Will you who dare, use one, or two...or all?

Make up your mind to Dare. These ideas aren't
worth a thing to you unless carried out. The 20th
Century Limited would stand forever in the station
if they didn't give it steam. Unless you dare, you
are on a dead center. How would you expect your
ship to come in if you never sent one out? It was
ridiculous for David to fight Goliath. Foolishness
for Columbus to try to sail around the earth. Nonsense for the Wright Brothers to dream they could
fly. *But suppose they hadn't tried?*

Master the five previous chapters. Who will be
content today without striving for all that the four-
square life has to offer—physical strength, mental
alertness, a magnetic personality, and a religion
that fits us for the highest service?

Achieve Greatly through a clear and powerful
urge to accomplish something notable; through a
superior persistence; through marked faith in yourself: "I can do great things if I try;" high capacity
for self-improvement; energy great enough to sus-
tain in long, tremendous drives; high enthusiasm;
intellectual curiosity — the itch to understand;
marked dexterity of eye, hand, tongue, and body;

creative imagination. These are some of Professor
Pitkin's thoughts which, coupled with his definition
of Achievement will open up vast possibilities.
"Achievement is distinguished successful endeavor,
usually in the face of difficulties. As such it always
possesses two characteristics; first, a certain supe-
riority of aim, and, secondly, exceptional skill in
execution."

*Never give up until you have released your
unused capacities for service and shared your gifts
with others.* One enkindled spirit can set hundreds
on fire.

I want to lift you to your peak performance
whatever that is. I want you to do some long-range
thinking, to have an imagination to see far beyond
anything I have said. If only one in a thousand gets
the big idea of a Dare, then I should be happy. I
know I would if that one were my own boy. We
haven't scratched the surface of human reservoirs
yet. Do you wonder that I'm urging you to Dare?
Picture anyone looking at the rushing, tumbling
waters of Niagara Falls—power beyond imagination even—and saying, "I'll take a cupful." Or that
echo of a little midget purring, "Just a thimbleful
for me." Oftentimes I find myself offering up a
prayer, "Lord, open the eyes of the blind, quicken
the imagination of the weak."

I read a part of the manuscript of "I Dare You"
to a young friend. "How very interesting," he said.

Gosh! If I've spent my time writing this to no greater purpose than interesting somebody, then I've miserably failed. Unless this book stirs you to Action and makes you want to get somewhere, then the daring adventure of magnificent four-square living has been presented by a mighty poor salesman.

ENVOI

Just a final word to you who have read "I Dare You": If you don't DARE, then it must be pretty much my fault. But you MUST DARE. You must do something. You can't put this book down without determining in a personal way to start something. Others have grown by DARING. So must you. It's time for ACTION for you. Come on. What's your DARE?

I DARE AND SHARE

It is my hope that every reader has gotten something out of the preceding chapters. Even if some haven't, I'm not going to give up. For a number of years in my business, we have been setting goals. Some didn't relish the idea at first. Bill didn't like to take a personal inventory. Mary didn't want to set a goal and then be urged to reach it. But many of those very ones who disliked the idea most have received the most benefit. The fact is that those who have set goals have advanced far more than the lukewarm or the belligerent. I have observed that setting a goal makes no appeal to the mediocre. But to those fired with an ambition really to achieve greatly, setting a goal becomes a program that stirs the inner soul to action.

If you have that urge to go a step farther, I want you to go back to pages 35, 62, 79 and 91 and check over your Physical, Mental, Social and Religious Dares. In daring to "Beat Your Best," you are going to need all sides of your checker.

With grim determination plan the most healthful, most thrilling, most romantic and most spiritual year of your life.

Let me sound a warning. A Dare based on half facts and only half thought through is less than half a Dare. Build your Dare in your own way, but do it seriously face to face with yourself—alone.

Don't be tempted to Dare beyond your capacity. That may entail disappointment and discouragement. On the other hand, make your Dare worthy of your best. The ambitious son of a cart horse never wins in the Derby races. Only thoroughbreds dominate there.

There is another admonition I would like to give to you eager crusaders now starting out on a daring program. There are two great parts to any program —the start and the finish. You have made your start and I want to urge you to finish. Industry, the professions, the world, are crying for men who can finish things. A friend told me the following incident:

"Last fall I saw a horse race at the Nebraska State Fair. A white-faced horse got the pole and took the lead. At the quarter he struck mud and the second horse passed him. I wish you could have seen that white-faced horse run the last half mile. The finish was close, but he won."

You are going to start this race on a high crest of enthusiasm. You are going to strike mud. Some are going to pass you, but during that last half mile run as you never ran before. It's down that last stretch that you white-faced horses must run home with everything that's in you.

In order to make your Dares definite, write them down. Fix a date for their accomplishment. With that courageous spirit which banishes all fear, you must reach your goal.

Finally, if this Dare program has helped you, why not pass it along to others.

I don't want you just to distribute a book. I want you to stimulate a life. If the Dare idea is worth anything it will grow through your influence and mine.

The first fourteen editions of "I Dare You" have been exhausted. The books were distributed by business executives to their employees, by colleges, schools, Y. M. C. A.'s, Scouts and from friend to friend. They have been circulated by those who have taken a Dare. Thus far an "I Dare You" Committee has handled the distribution.

This book is my contribution to the development of the youth of our land. I do not want any royalties or profit from it. Whatever amounts are received for it through the "I Dare You" Committee after all expenses are paid will go to some worthy Youth cause.

"I Dare You" Clubs, "I Dare You" Days, "I Dare You" Programs are becoming popular. If you count yourself among those who have Dared, then you will begin to share the "I Dare You" life with others.

Now that you have read this book, what are you going to do about it?

You with an Ambition on Fire—

You with a Brilliant Career before you—

You with Creative Ability as yet untapped—

You with an Executive Mind destined to carry you far—

You who have already Dared but haven't as yet learned to Share—

What are YOU going to do right now to lift yourself out of the crowd and make something significant out of your life?

In the pages that follow, men who have achieved tell how the "I Dare You" spirit has gripped them. In your own place, in your own way, you can lift yourself and be a part of a recognized Daring group.

Will you Dare yourself?

Will you pass the Dare spirit along to others?

What you do *today* and in the immediate days that follow is the thing that will prove whether or not you possess the spirit of the priceless few who DARE.

WM. H. DANFORTH.

CPSIA information can be obtained
at www.ICGtesting.com
Printed in the USA
BVOW08s1814301017
499009BV00003B/199/P